The Redneck Cookbook

The Redneck Cookbook

134 Mighty Fine Down Home Recipes—
Complete With All the Trimmin's

LO'RETTA LOVE

Illustrations by Ernie Eldredge

BLACK DOG
& LEVENTHAL
PUBLISHERS
NEW YORK

PUBLISHED BY

Black Dog & Leventhal Publishers, Inc.
151 West 19th Street
New York, NY 10011

DISTRIBUTED BY

Workman Publishing Company
708 Broadway
New York, NY 10003

Designed by Martin Lubin Graphic Design

Manufactured in the United States of America

ISBN 1-884822-69-X

h g f e d c b a

Library of Congress Cataloging-in-Publication Data
Love, Lo'retta.
   The Redneck cookbook : 134 mighy fine down home recipes—complete with all the trimmin's / by Lo'retta Love.
      p. cm.
   ISBN 1-884822-69-X
   1. Cookery, American—Southern style.   2. Rednecks.   I.
Title.
TX715.2.S68L7   1997
641.5975—dc21

                                        96-53240
                                        CIP

Contents

Introduction

My Dear Cousin Nadine,

I am glad to know that you and Dwayne are fully recovered from your wedding festivities. Your Uncle Merle and Daddy had great intentions of making one of those video cassettes, but neither one didn't have any idea how to turn the darned camera on!

Now, seeing that you was in such a tizzy about gettin' married that you might not remember what was served, your mama, aunties, cousins, and a passel of neighbors from Reed Hooker Road put together these recipes. They pretty much include some stuff from your wedding, and a few surprises that us married folk want to share with you. Before too long you should be cooking up some mighty fine fixins' for Dwayne because he's got a taste for chicken and taters and bacon and just about anything else he can get down his gullet.

Nadine, let me just tell you details about the wedding that you might have missed. Right from the get go there was hootin' and hollerin' when the finger foods came out: Mock Oysters Rockerfeller that looked so fancy; and delicious Peanut Butter and Bacon Bites. No sooner had people got to work on the Paw Paw Pâté, then out came the Wild Turkey fresh killed (straight from the yard). Chicken came out every which way—Dixie Grilled, à la King, and International—so fancy looking you'd have sworn it was French.

Next came the meat. The hollering of "Pass me this!" and "Give me that!" got louder than a freight train, especially by your five brothers. You know how they like it—real rich, meaty, and dripping with gravy. Virginia Corn Scrapple and Mama's Meat Loaf come to mind—it was a real free-for-all.

Fish was mighty good too—Vesta's Tuna Noodle Casserole was about the best I ever tasted. I don't want Merle or your daddy to know I'm telling you about fish or else they will start in with those fishing stories and never stop. By the time we got to the vegetables, we were on a roll. You should have seen them getting at that Fried Corn, Ham Hocks and Greens, and Cabbage with Beer and Bouillon. Did someone say finger lickin'good?

Then came the big finale—store-bought wedding cake. Personally, I was thinking, who needs store-bought cake anyhow when you have a table full of Mississippi Mud Cake, In-the-Pink Marshmallow Puddin', and Chocolate Twinkie Pie.

Now let me give you some good wedding advice: cooking isn't something you measure. It's something you feel. It's like an instinct. Never be afraid to try domething different. If you don't have wine for a sauce, try a little Coca-Cola. Make it look pretty and serve it up right. Don't let Junior eat from the can, make him a sandwich from one of the many recipes I've sent you here. Cook with your heart and your stomach and wash everything down with plenty of these great beverages we have given you here.

Your lovin' cousin,

Lo'retta

Starters and Finger Foods

Nothing goes so well with entertaining as a little treat for your guests that keeps them busy, and buys you a little more time in the kitchen getting dinner ready. A lot of the recipes that follow are perfect for that, and many can be made up completely in advance such as Celia's Spread, Ms. Patty's Pâté, Paw Paw's Pâté, and Volcano Cheese Ball. Most of the rest can be pretty much prepared in advance and cooked—or given a little last-minute warming—just before your company arrives.

Black Bean Nachos

SERVES 6

A little messy, but great for entertaining if you aren't too fussy about your carpet.

½ medium onion, diced
3 tablespoons butter
2 15-ounce cans black beans
¼ cup chili powder
¼ cup ground cumin
1 tablespoon salt
1 teaspoon black pepper
1 large bag tortilla chips
1 8-ounce bag (2 cups) grated cheddar cheese
1 8-ounce jar tomato salsa
½ of a 12-ounce jar pickled jalapeño slices
½ cup sour cream

Preheat oven to 400 degrees. Cook onion in butter until soft. Mix together onion, black beans, chili powder, cumin, salt, and pepper. Place chips on an oven-proof serving platter and cover with black bean mixture. Top with cheese and bake until cheese is melted. Remove from oven and pour salsa all over and sprinkle with the jalapeño slices. Serve with sour cream.

Celia's Spread

SERVES 8

Now I know this sounds a little foo-foo, but try it and I guarantee you and your guests will love it!

1 8-ounce package cream cheese
⅓ cup A–1® steak sauce
½ 8-ounce bottle Major Grey's chutney
Waverly Wafers®

Place the cream cheese in the center of a serving platter. Pour A–1 over the top and let it run down the sides. Top with the chutney and serve with Waverly Wafers.

Endless Bacon Wraps

SERVES 35 TO 40 PEOPLE

Everyone always has bacon. Wrap it around anything for a great treat. That is why I say endless, because you can substitute anything for the water chestnuts: chicken livers, pitted prunes, canned pineapple, cooked vegetables, potato chunks...endless!

2 10-ounce cans water chestnuts, drained
1 5-ounce bottle soy sauce
brown sugar
1 pound sliced bacon

Marinate chestnuts in soy sauce for at least an hour, turning a lot. Remove chestnuts from marinade and roll in brown sugar. Wrap each chestnut in half a strip of raw bacon and secure it with a toothpick. Bake in a preheated 400-degree oven for about 15 minutes, or until bacon is crispy. Serve 'em hot.

Clammy Crackers

SERVES 8

Ritz crackers spread with this hot, cheese-topped dip are something else.

1 stick (½ cup) oleo
1 onion, chopped
½ green bell pepper, chopped
½ teaspoon garlic powder
1 teaspoon fresh parsley, chopped
2 teaspoons dried oregano
½ teaspoon Tabasco®
¼ teaspoon cayenne pepper
¼ teaspoon black pepper
2 6½-ounce cans chopped clams
1 teaspoon lemon juice
½ cup bread crumbs
4 slices Velveeta® cheese
2 tablespoons Parmesan cheese
Ritz® crackers

Preheat oven to 375 degrees. In a pot simmer butter, onions, green pepper, garlic powder, parsley, oregano, Tabasco, cayenne, and black pepper for 5 minutes or until onions and peppers are soft. Remove from heat and add clams with their liquid and the lemon juice. Add enough bread crumbs until mixture kinda looks like oatmeal. Put into a baking dish and top with Velveeta. Sprinkle with Parmesan and bake for 20 minutes, or until cheese is bubbly. Serve with Ritz crackers.

Cocktail Meatballs

MAKES ENOUGH FOR A RALLY!

You can use ground chuck with a lot of salt and pepper added in place of sausage if you like.

1½ pounds sausage
1 12-ounce bottle chili sauce
1 12-ounce jar red currant jelly

Make bite-size sausage balls and brown well in a small amount of fat. Drain real good. In a pot, mix the chili sauce and the jelly; heat this up a bit and add sausage balls. Simmer until the sauce gets nice and thick. Keep warm in a chafing dish and use toothpicks to spear balls.

Gourmet Ice Pickle Sticks

MAKES 1 QUART

Make this up and you'll have enough for a few days' snacks.

1 quart whole dill pickles, drained (but reserve the juice)
4 garlic cloves
1 cup sugar

Drain dill pickles, reserving juice, and quarter. Place garlic cloves in bottom of the pickle jar, then put quartered pickles back in the jar. Pour sugar on top of the pickles. Shake the jar over and back to mix sugar over pickles and let set out on the counter for 1 hour. Cover pickles with reserved liquid and refrigerate for at least 3 days before serving.

Mock Oysters Rockerfeller

SERVES 8

This recipe can be doubled for a big crowd. If your supermarket doesn't carry garlic cheese, substitute any herbed cheese.

2 10-ounce packages frozen spinach
1 medium onion, chopped up
1 stick (½ cup) oleo
1 10¾-ounce can cream of mushroom soup
1 4-ounce can chopped mushrooms
1 roll (4 ounces) Kraft garlic cheese
Fritos®

Boil spinach and drain it good. Cook onions in oleo until they are soft. Mix up soup, onions, mushrooms, and mix with spinach and crumbled cheese in pan. Keep hot and let cheese melt. Serve from a chafing dish with Fritos for dipping.

Ms. Patty's Pâté

SERVES 8

Ms. Patty makes this for the men she is courting, and she courts a lot of 'em. So she likes this recipe because it's easy to make and after the evening she can smooth it over and top with more olives, and stick it back in the fridge for the next fool!

½ pound liverwurst
1 3-ounce package cream cheese
1 stick (½ cup) soft butter
2 teaspoons Worcestershire sauce
¼ teaspoon Tabasco®
¼ cup chopped black olives

Put all ingredients except the olives in a bowl and mix up until smooth. Spoon this into a mold (Ms. Patty uses a heart-shaped one) sprayed with Pam. Refrigerate until thoroughly chilled. Unmold on top of a plate lined with a leaf of lettuce. Top with chopped olives.

Paw Paw's Pâté

SERVES 8

This is lovely to bring out for guests, and you won't believe how simple it is to make.

1 log (8 ounces) liverwurst
¼ cup finely chopped pistachio nuts
Ritz® crackers
parsley sprigs

Carefully remove wrapper from liverwurst log. Spread pistachios on wax paper and gently roll liverwurst log in them until it is covered all over. Place on a plate and surround with Ritz crackers and decorate with parsley sprigs.

Peanut Butter & Bacon Bites

MAKES 24 BITES

Make plenty as they "sell like hot cakes."

1 cup creamy peanut butter
¼ cup crumbled bacon bits
6 slices rye bread, toasted
peanuts in the shell for garnishing the serving plate

Mix peanut butter until slightly softened. Add bacon bits and blend it up good. Spread mixture on top of toasts and warm in the oven so the peanut butter will get even creamier. Cut each slice into four triangles. Place the bites on a plate garnished with peanuts in the shell.

Sardines Supreme

SERVES 6

This one is for sardine lovers only.

3 slices bread, crusts removed and each one halved diagonally
1 3¾-ounce tin sardine fillets
2 teaspoons minced onion
1 teaspoon whole-grain mustard
3 tablespoons butter
1 teaspoon vinegar
¼ teaspoon salt
1 lemon

Preheat broiler and toast bread triangles. In a bowl, mix 5 sardine fillets with onions, mustard, butter,
vinegar, and salt. Spread over
toasted triangles. Top each half with one whole sardine fillet and
squeeze a little lemon juice on top. Broil until they are warm, about
30 seconds, and serve immediately.

Tamale Dip

SERVES 12

Tamales, Tabasco, chili sauce, and chili powder make this a spicy dip,
perfect for a crowd.

2 medium onions, chopped up
1 28-ounce can crushed tomatoes
1 14-ounce can tomato sauce
1 clove garlic, minced
2 large cans tamales, chopped up
dash Tabasco®

1½ tablespoons chili sauce
1 can black olives, drained and chopped
salt, black pepper, and chili powder, how you like it
grated cheddar cheese
corn chips

Mix onions, tomatoes, tomato sauce, and garlic in a pot and cook on low heat, uncovered, for 30 minutes. Add the chopped tamales, and don't forget to throw in the sauce from the cans. Add all the other ingredients except the cheese and corn chips and cook for an additional 15 minutes over low heat, stirring. Transfer mixture to a baking dish and sprinkle the top with grated cheddar cheese. Bake in a preheated 350-degree oven for 10 minutes or until heated through and cheese is melted. Serve hot with corn chips.

Stuffed Mushrooms

SERVES 8

This recipe works well with any size mushroom—some prefer the larger ones, some like the smaller bite-size ones.

1 pound mushrooms
½ pound hot sausage
American cheese slices

Preheat oven to 375 degrees. Remove stems from mushrooms and wash the caps. Fill empty hole in each cap with sausage. Place mushrooms on top of broiler pan. Bake mushrooms until sausage is cooked through, approximately 20 minutes. Remove pan from oven and turn off the oven. Cover mushrooms with American cheese. Put pan back in oven until cheese melts. Drain mushrooms on paper towels and serve warm.

Volcano Cheese Ball

SERVES 8 AS A BEFORE-DINNER SNACK.

Substitute cheddar cheese for Tally Ho cheese if your supermarket doesn't carry this specific brand.

1 pound Tally Ho® cheese
1 8-ounce package cream cheese
1 stick (½ cup) butter
½ small onion, grated
2 tablespoons Worcestershire sauce
¼ cup white wine
dash Tabasco®
barbecue sauce
ground pecans

Let the cheeses set out until the chill is out. Place all ingredients except barbecue sauce and pecans in a mixer bowl and blend at medium speed until smooth. Work the cheese mixture into a ball and refrigerate until firm. Make a hole in the center of the ball and fill with barbecue sauce. Smooth cheese over the top of the barbecue sauce and then put it back in the refrigerator. Before serving, roll cheese ball in ground pecans to coat and put it on a plate surrounded with crackers.

Soups and Stews

I have heard that people, they say in England or somewhere, actually drink tea. I don't mean iced tea. I mean hot tea from a cup. Don't get me wrong, I have had occasion to drink hot tea from a cup, but let me tell you, that sure wasn't that fancy "orange pekoe" we were swigging. No way. The point I'm trying to make is that those English folks sit down to four o'clock tea and the whole world turns all loverly. So how about sitting yourself right down at four o'clock and diggin' into something with a little more meat on its bones, like a good ol' bowl of soup. Talk about the world goin' all loverly, will you? (By the way, if you're curious about difference between a soup and a stew, here it is: If a fork can stand up straight in the bowl, then it's a stew. If a spoon stands up then it's soup.)

If you like country cooking, you'll find a lot of the classics here—split-pea soup, peanut soup, gumbo, and jambalaya, just to name a few—though spiced a bit more mildly than some folks might like them. Other recipes, however, rely a bit more heavily on convenience foods like condensed soup and canned vegetables, and that suits some just fine, too. But remember that soup and stew making is not a science, so feel free to make substitutions and additions to please yourself.

Celery Soup

SERVES 8

An easy dress-up for good old canned celery soup. It works pretty good with cream of asparagus soup, too, if that's not too fancy for you.

4 10¾-ounce cans condensed cream of celery soup
8 strips bacon, fried crisp
4 hard-boiled eggs, grated
fresh parsley, chopped

Pour soup into a large saucepan and slowly add one can of water for each can of soup, stirring constantly. Crumble bacon and add to soup along with grated hard-boiled eggs. Heat. Sprinkle with parsley and serve.

Chicken Jambalaya

SERVES 8

This is a simple version of the chicken-and-rice favorite. Some folks spice theirs up a bit more, and you can, too, if you feel like it.

1 3-pound chicken
¼ cup lard
½ pound raw ham, diced
⅓ cup diced onion
½ cup diced tomato
1 cup uncooked rice
1 bay leaf
¼ teaspoon thyme
¼ cup chopped fresh parsley
1 teaspoon salt
¼ teaspoon black pepper

Cut chicken into 8 pieces. Heat lard in a skillet and sauté chicken and ham for 5 minutes. Remove the meat from the pan. Sauté the onion and tomato in the same skillet for 3 minutes. Stir in the rice.

When the rice is well-coated with lard, return the chicken and ham to the skillet. Cover these ingredients with boiling water. Add bay leaf, thyme, parsley, salt, and pepper. Simmer, uncovered, until chicken is tender and rice is done, about 45 minutes. Dry out the jambalaya by placing it, uncovered, for 5 minutes or more in a preheated 350-degree oven.

Chicken Okra Gumbo

SERVES 8

This is a popular way to use home-canned tomatoes and okra, but store-bought canned tomatoes and frozen okra work well, too.

2½- to 3-pound chicken
oil
flour
1 quart (4 cups) canned tomatoes, chopped
1 quart (4 cups) canned okra, left whole
1 large onion, chopped
3 bay leaves
salt and black pepper to taste

Cut chicken into 8 individual parts and heat oil in a deep kettle. Fry chicken until lightly browned. Remove chicken pieces from pan (leave the oil from the fried chicken in the kettle) and put chicken into one gallon of boiling water. Boil until very tender, about 1 hour. While chicken is boiling, add enough flour to the oil the chicken was fried in to make a paste. Cook the paste over medium heat for 3 minutes, stirring constantly, and set aside. Remove chicken from water; pick meat from bones and dice. Add chicken, tomatoes and okra with their liquid, and flour paste into the broth the chicken boiled in. Add onion and bay leaves. Cook slowly, uncovered, for 4 hours. Season with salt and pepper. Serve over white rice.

Cold Tomato and Cottage Cheese Soup

SERVES 6

If you want a rich, cold soup, give this one a try—it's a good recipe for those hot days when you don't even want to turn the stove on.

1 10¾-ounce can condensed tomato soup
1 pint (2 cups) coffee cream (half-and-half)
1 teaspoon lemon juice
1 teaspoon horseradish
few drops Tabasco®
½ cup creamed cottage cheese
¼ cup chopped green onions (scallions)
salt and black pepper to taste
sour cream and parsley sprigs for garnish

Put tomato soup, coffee cream, lemon juice, horseradish, and Tabasco in a bowl. Beat with a hand mixer until well mixed and smooth. Add cottage cheese and green onions and stir until mixed. Season with salt and pepper and chill. Serve in cold bowls and top each with a dollop of sour cream and a sprig of parsley.

Corn Soup

SERVES 6

This recipe calls for fresh corn, but you can substitute frozen or canned corn (drain it well) if you must.

¼ cup minced onion
½ stick (¼ cup) butter
1 tablespoon lemon juice
½ teaspoon dry mustard
1 teaspoon sugar
1 teaspoon salt
½ teaspoon black pepper
2 cups fresh raw corn
2 cups chicken stock
2 cups coffee cream (half-and-half)
dash Tabasco®

Sauté onion in butter until transparent. Mix in lemon juice, mustard, sugar, salt, and pepper. Add corn and chicken stock. Bring to a boil, cover, reduce heat, and simmer for about 10 minutes. At serving time, add cream and Tabasco and heat but do not allow the soup to boil.

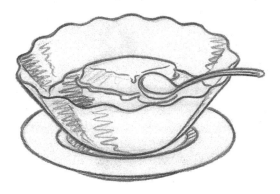

Cream of Peanut Soup

SERVES 8

This variation of the southern favorite uses tomato and whipping cream.

1 stick (½ cup) butter
2 stalks celery, chopped
1 onion, chopped
1 tablespoon flour
½ gallon (8 cups) chicken broth
1½ cups chunky peanut butter
1 cup diced tomato
2 cups whipping cream
fresh parsley for garnish

Melt butter in a pan and cook celery and onion until transparent. Add flour and stir until well blended. Add the chicken broth and bring to a boil. Stir in the peanut butter until melted. Add tomatoes. Add the cream, heat thoroughly, and serve garnished with parsley.

Fast Spinach Soup

SERVES 5

Don't overlook baby food as a real time saver—it works great in this fast, rich soup.

2 large jars spinach junior baby food
4 cups chicken broth
2 cups canned or homemade white sauce
1 teaspoon curry powder
2 hard-boiled eggs, chopped

Mix well all ingredients except eggs and heat in the top of a double boiler set over simmering water. Serve hot, garnished with hard-boiled egg.

Football Game Stew

SERVES 8

The tapioca in this recipe thickens the gravy.

2 pounds round steak or stew meat, cut into 1-inch cubes
1 28-ounce can crushed tomatoes
1 small can peas
2 carrots, cut into rounds
2 onions, quartered
2 potatoes, cubed
1 green bell pepper, diced
¼ cup raw minute tapioca
¼ cup bread crumbs
1 tablespoon Worcestershire sauce
½ teaspoon garlic salt
1 bay leaf
¼ teaspoon thyme
¼ teaspoon oregano
¼ teaspoon basil
salt and black pepper
1 tablespoon lemon juice

Preheat oven to 250 degrees. Place all ingredients except lemon juice in a large casserole and cover with water. Bake uncovered 4 to 5 hours. Meat will brown while cooking. If necessary, add more water. Add lemon juice just before serving.

Ground Beef Vegetable Soup

MAKES A POT THAT WILL SERVE 8 TO 10

A little bit of everything finds its way into this soup. Don't be afraid to make some additions or substitutions of your own.

1 pound ground beef
1 medium onion, diced
1 slice bacon
2 8-ounce cans tomato sauce
1 14.5-ounce can diced tomatoes
2 15-ounce cans mixed vegetables, drained
1 cup frozen corn
2 to 3 red potatoes, diced
2 tablespoons uncooked rice
¼ cup broken spaghetti noodles
1 handful macaroni
2 bay leaves
¼ teaspoon thyme
¼ teaspoon oregano
2 quarts (8 cups) water
salt and pepper to taste

Brown ground beef with onion; drain. Mix beef and all remaining ingredients in a large pot. Simmer until potatoes are cooked and soup is seasoned, about an hour.

Navy Bean Soup

SERVES 8

Cooking times vary greatly with beans, so be sure to watch them and adjust the cooking time accordingly.

2 cups dried navy beans

2 ham shanks
8 cups water
6 celery stalks, chopped
2 onions, chopped
2 cups canned tomatoes
salt and black pepper to taste

Soak beans overnight in water to cover. Cover shanks with the cold water in large soup kettle and simmer 2 to 3 hours. Add drained beans, celery, onions, and tomatoes to pot in which shanks have been simmering and cook approximately 1½ hours longer, or until beans are very tender. Season with salt and pepper to taste.

Seven-Can Soup

SERVES 6

*This soup is poured over toasted bread and sautéed chicken breasts,
although for a lighter meal you could leave all that out and just serve it
on its own.*

1 10-ounce can chicken broth
1 10.5-ounce can chicken gumbo
1 10-ounce can beef bouillon
1 herb bunch (whatever you have around)
2 tablespoons chopped fresh parsley
1 10-ounce package frozen mixed vegetables
1 3-ounce can B in B® chopped mushrooms
1 onion, chopped
4 tablespoons butter
1½ to 2 cans small whole peeled
potatoes, sliced
2 tablespoons bacon fat
1 cup solid-pack canned tomatoes
1 pound boneless, skinless chicken
breasts
sliced French bread, buttered and
toasted

Put chicken broth, chicken gumbo,
beef bouillon, herb bunch, and parsley
into a large soup pot and simmer slowly
for 15 minutes. Add mixed vegetables and mushrooms with their juice. Sauté onion in butter until gold-
en and add it to the soup along with the tomatoes. Fry potatoes in
bacon fat for 5 to 10 minutes and add to soup. Let soup simmer,
uncovered, 30 minutes. Meanwhile, sauté chicken breasts in butter
until cooked through. Place slices of toasted French bread in bottom
of soup plates. Place chicken breasts on top of bread and pour soup
over all and serve.

Split Pea Soup

MAKES 3½ QUARTS

You can substitute cooked, chopped ham for the frankfurters in this soup or leave out the meat altogether if you like.

2 cups dried green split peas
2 quarts water
1 whole ham hock, split
10 peppercorns
3 carrots, sliced
½ cup chopped onion
2 cups chopped celery
2 tablespoons chopped fresh parsley
2 Kosher-style frankfurters, sliced
1 cup milk
1 cup beef bouillon
salt to taste

Soak peas in 2 quarts water overnight. Bring soaked peas to a boil in the water they soaked in. Reduce heat, add ham hock and peppercorns, and simmer, covered, for 1 hour. Add carrots, onions, celery, and parsley and cook until vegetables are tender. Add frankfurters, milk, and bouillon and simmer for 20 minutes more. Add salt to taste.

White Velvet Soup

Finely chopped almonds and bread crumbs are unusual thickners in this soup.

1 large hen
2 quarts (8 cups) water
2 tablespoons minced onion
2 bunches celery, cut up
2 sprigs fresh parsley
1 clove
1 cup almonds, finely chopped
2 cups fine white bread crumbs
pinch nutmeg
pinch cayenne pepper
1 pint (2 cups) whipping cream
salt to taste

In a large kettle, bring hen and water, covered, to a simmer. Add onion, celery, parsley, and clove. When hen is tender (about 2 hours), remove it from stock. Remove the breast meat from the hen and chop it fine. Strain stock, discard the vegetables, and put it back in the kettle. Add 1 cup of the chopped chicken breast, the almonds, bread crumbs, nutmeg, cayenne, cream, and salt. Bring soup to a boil and serve with toast or crackers.

Wine Soup

This wine soup, flavored with sage, lemon, and cinnamon, should be served ice cold. Be sure to taste it just before serving and season it with a little salt if you feel it needs it.

1 tablespoon dried sage leaves
4 cups claret wine
2 cups water
1 lemon, sliced thin
1 tablespoon broken cinnamon stick
1 tablespoon sugar
2 egg yolks, well beaten

Cook sage in 1 cup of boiling water until tender; as water evaporates, add more. In another pot, bring wine, water, lemon, cinnamon, and sugar to a boil and cook until sugar is dissolved. Add sage, let boil, and pour while very hot slowly over well-beaten yolks. Strain and chill. Serve ice cold.

Meat

You don't have to do much to a beautiful steak, but fancy high-priced meats is not what this chapter is about. The recipes that follow will show you how to cook your bargain cuts of meat and make them tender and tasty, too. And when it comes to ground meat, you'll find many ways to use that if you have a hankering for something more than just a plain old burger. But beef is not the only kind of meat we're talking about here. Don't forget pork, ham, and sausage; a lot of recipes here tell you just what folks like to do with them, too.

Bacon Gourmet

SERVES 2 AS A SIDE DISH

Theres nothing like a side of this bacon dish to pick up your eggs in the morning, or your fish or greens any time of day.

1 teaspoon mustard
2 teaspoons Worcestershire sauce
1 egg yolk
6 thin slices bacon
bread crumbs

Preheat oven to 250 degrees. In a small bowl, whisk together mustard, Worcestershire, and egg yolk. Dip bacon in yolk mixture, then roll in bread crumbs. Lay on cookie sheet and bake in preheated oven for 20 minutes, or until bacon is crispy.

Barbecued Wieners

MAKES 3 SERVINGS

Serve these on buns to your crew watching the game.

6 wieners
3 tablespoons butter
½ cup chopped onion
1 8-ounce can tomato sauce
4 teaspoons sugar
3 tablespoons vinegar
4 teaspoons Worcestershire sauce
1 teaspoon mustard
½ teaspoon black pepper
1 teaspoon paprika

Preheat oven to 350 degrees. Boil wieners for 10 minutes, then split them lengthwise and place in greased baking dish. Brown the onions in a skillet with the butter. Add the remaining ingredients and bring to a boil. Pour the sauce over the wieners and bake for 30 minutes.

Chicken-Fried Steak

SERVES 6

Be sure to see the Leftover Chicken-Fried Steak Sandwich recipe (see page 88). If you're lucky, you may find yourself with a little extra of this delicacy in your icebox.

1½ to 2 pounds round steak
2 eggs
2 tablespoons milk
1 cup flour
1 teaspoon salt
1 teaspoon black pepper
Crisco® or vegetable oil for frying

Trim and cut round steak into individual serving pieces. Pound steak thoroughly with a meat pounder, rolling pin, or heavy pot; try to get it down to half its thickness. In a small bowl, beat eggs and milk. Season flour with salt and pepper and place on a plate. Put ⅓ to ½ inch fat in the bottom of a heavy skillet large enough to hold meat in a single layer (or you can use two skillets) and set over medium heat. Dip meat into egg mixture, then into flour; transfer meat to hot skillet and brown slowly on both sides. Reduce heat to low, cover skillet tightly, and cook meat over low heat 45 to 60 minutes, or until tender.

Chilicornghetti

This casserole can be prepared up to baking and refrigerated up to two days.

2 tablespoons vegetable shortening
½ pound uncooked vermicelli, broken into 1-inch pieces
2 pounds ground chuck
2 cloves garlic, minced
2 cups chopped onions
2 cups chopped celery
½ cup chopped green bell pepper
1 17-ounce can whole-kernel corn and liquid
1 tablespoon salt
1 teaspoon black pepper
1 tablespoon chili powder
1 28-ounce can Italian plum tomatoes and liquid
1 cup grated sharp cheddar cheese

Over high heat, melt shortening in a 5-quart pot. Sauté vermicelli until it is a nutty brown color, stirring often. Add ground chuck and brown it, stirring occasionally. Reduce heat to medium-low and add all remaining ingredients except cheese. Cover and cook slowly for 25 minutes, stirring occasionally. Before serving, preheat oven to 350 degrees. Place mixture in a large casserole, sprinkle cheese on top, and bake, uncovered, for 25 minutes or until cheese is melted and sauce is bubbling up around the edges.

Curried Round Steak

You make the gravy for this spicy meat stew in the same pan it bakes in, and that's real convenient.

¼ pound salt pork, diced
2 pounds round steak, cut into 1-inch cubes
3 small onions, diced
1 tablespoon curry powder
salt and black pepper to taste
¼ cup milk
2 heaping tablespoons flour

Fry salt pork in skillet over high heat until the fat is rendered. Add diced steak and brown. Add onions, curry powder, salt, and pepper and cook for 5 minutes. Transfer to a covered roaster, cover with hot water and cook, covered, until meat is tender, about 1½ hours. Whisk together flour and milk. Push meat to one side of the roaster and whisk milk into pan juices. Cook over high heat, stirring constantly, until gravy is thickened. Serve over rice.

Fancy Hamburgers

MAKES 6

Mashed potatoes are a natural to serve with these fancy, fixed-up burgers.

2 pounds ground beef
¼ cup (½ stick) butter
2 medium onions, chopped
¼ pound mushrooms, chopped
½ teaspoon dried thyme
¼ teaspoon dried rosemary
¼ teaspoon coarsely ground black pepper
½ teaspoon salt
¾ cup sherry
¼ cup water

Shape ground beef into 6 patties. Broil in skillet until brown and cooked to taste. Meanwhile, melt butter in small saucepan and add onions, mushrooms, and spices. Sauté over medium heat until vegetables are golden brown. Add sherry and water. Bring to a boil and simmer, uncovered, for 5 minutes. Serve sauce over hamburgers.

Hot Tamale Pie

SERVES 10

This recipe calls for cooking chuck roast in water until tender and then passing it through a meat grinder. If you don't have a grinder, allow the meat to cool for a while and then shred it finely with your fingers— you'll just have a slightly different texture to your pie than if you had used a meat grinder.

6 pounds chuck roast
1 6-ounce can tomato paste
¼ teaspoon cayenne pepper
3½ teaspoons salt
1 teaspoon cumin
1½ cups cornmeal
4 teaspoons flour
3 teaspoons chili powder
1½ cup cold water
2½ cups chicken broth
paprika

Place meat in a large kettle and add water to cover. Bring to a boil, reduce heat, cover, and simmer for 3 hours or until meat begins to fall off the bone. Remove meat and reserve the cooking liquid. Grind meat in a meat grinder and add enough cooking liquid to moisten well (about 1 cup). Add tomato paste, cayenne, 1½ teaspoons of the salt, and cumin. Set aside. Make a mush by mixing cornmeal, flour, chili powder, and the remaining 2 teaspoons of salt with the cold water. In a medium saucepan, heat chicken broth until boiling. Stir cornmeal mixture into broth and cook, stirring constantly, until thickened, about 10 minutes. Preheat oven to 350 degrees and grease a large rectangular casserole dish. Pour a layer of mush into the casserole, reserving enough to cover the top. Add meat mixture and top with the remaining mush. Dust with paprika. Bake until hot and bubbly.

Italian Liver and Onions

SERVES 6

Men love this one!

1 pound liver, thinly sliced
salt and pepper to taste
½ cup dry red wine
6 tablespoons olive oil
4 medium onions, thinly sliced
1 cup flour, plus 1 tablespoon for gravy
salt and black pepper to taste
pinch of dried oregano

Let liver stand in wine for 1 hour or more in the icebox, turning it every once in a while.

Mix the flour and salt and pepper to taste and set aside. In a large skillet, cook onions in 4 tablespoons of the olive oil until they get nice and brown. Take onions out of the skillet and keep them hot. In the same skillet, add the remaining 2 tablespoons of olive oil. Drain liver, but save that wine! Season flour with salt and pepper; roll the liver in the flour. Add the liver to the skillet and brown it over medium-high heat, 3 to 4 minutes on each side, adding more oil if you need it. (If your skillet is too small to hold the liver in a single layer you may have to do this in two batches.) Remove liver from skillet and keep hot. Reduce heat to medium, add the remaining 1 tablespoon of flour, oregano, and reserved wine to skillet. Stir until it gets a little thick and season with salt and pepper to taste. Pour the hot gravy over the liver and onions.

Jellied Beef Loaf

SERVES 8

You may want to unmold this loaf on a platter lined with iceberg lettuce leaves and surround it with cherry tomatoes.

2 pounds round steak, cut into 1-inch cubes
1 onion, diced
2 stalks celery, diced
1 carrot, chopped
3 cups boiling water
a few sprigs parsley
1 cup tomato juice
1 tablespoon vinegar
2 teaspoons salt
1½ teaspoons gelatin
⅛ teaspoon black pepper
¼ teaspoon mustard powder
½ teaspoon Worcestershire sauce
1 teaspoon creamed-style horseradish
½ teaspoon vinegar

Place first nine ingredients in a kettle and simmer, covered, for 1½ hours. Drain, reserving liquid. Chop meat slightly. Cool ½ cup of reserved broth and soak gelatin in it for 5 minutes. In a medium saucepan, heat remaining broth (there should be about 3½ cups) until boiling. Dissolve gelatin mixture into hot broth. Remove from heat and add remaining ingredients. Transfer to a large bowl and refrigerate until it begins to thicken, about 1 to 1½ hours. Add meat to gelatin and pour into a large greased 3-quart mold; chill until firm, 6 hours or overnight. When ready to serve, dip bottom of mold in hot water for 15 seconds to loosen it and then turn mold out onto the center of a platter. Serve with more creamed horseradish on the side.

Mama's Meat Loaf

SERVES 6

This meat loaf gets its flavor from a combination of ground beef and ground sausage.

1 pound ground beef
¼ pound ground sausage
¼ cup cracker crumbs
2 medium onions, finely chopped
2 cloves garlic, minced
2 stalks celery, finely chopped
1 egg, lightly beaten
¼ cup milk
½ cup chili sauce
2 teaspoons salt
1 teaspoon Ac'cent®
½ teaspoon black pepper
1 8-ounce can tomato sauce

Preheat oven to 350 degrees. In a large bowl, thoroughly mix all the ingredients except the tomato sauce. Press the mixture into a well-greased loaf pan and bake for 1 hour. Pour tomato sauce over the top of the meat loaf and bake for another 15 minutes. To serve, take meatloaf out of the pan and place on a hot platter; pour tomato sauce over the top.

Macaroni Italienne

SERVES 6

Try this meaty variation on baked macaroni and cheese.

1 pound ground beef
1 large can mushrooms, drained and liquid reserved
8 strips bacon
1 large onion
1 28-ounce can crushed tomatoes
1 pound cheddar cheese, grated
garlic to taste
salt and black pepper to taste
½ pound package macaroni

Pour 1 quart cold water over ground beef and let it soak overnight in the icebox. The following morning, simmer beef and soaking water in a pot for one hour. Add juice from mushrooms and 2 cups of water and boil hard for another hour.

Fry bacon in a big skillet until crispy; remove bacon but save the grease. Fry the onion in the grease and add the tomatoes. Cook that until it turns to mush. Add the beef, beef juice, bacon (crumble it), cheese, garlic, salt and pepper, and mushrooms to the mush.

Meanwhile, preheat oven to 350 degrees. Cook macaroni in salted boiling water until done. Drain the macaroni well and add it to the beef mush. Pour into a casserole and bake until hot, about 30 minutes. Can be made a day ahead and reheated.

Marinated Flank Steak

SERVES 4

This recipe can easily be doubled for company.

¾ cup vegetable oil
2 tablespoons chopped onion
¼ cup soy sauce
½ cup honey
2 tablespoons vinegar
⅛ teaspoons powdered ginger
¼ teaspoon garlic salt
2 pounds flank steak

In a small bowl, combine all ingredients except flank steak and mix thoroughly. Place flank steak in a shallow pan and pour marinade over it. Cover and chill for at least 4 hours. Preheat broiler, discard marinade, and broil meat five minutes on each side or to taste. Cut into thin, diagonal strips and serve.

Oriental Ribs

SERVES 6 TO 8

These ribs are best grilled, but you can also do them under your broiler if you don't have a grill—just watch them closely.

5 pounds beef short ribs
1 cup burgundy wine
1¼ cups soy sauce
¼ cup sugar
1 cup applesauce
1 teaspoon garlic powder
½ teaspoon powdered ginger
1 teaspoon meat tenderizer

In a large kettle or Dutch oven, boil ribs in salted water to cover for about 15 minutes or until tender. Drain, discard liquid, and slice into 1-rib sections. In a large bowl, combine burgundy, soy sauce, sugar, applesauce, garlic powder, ginger, and meat tenderizer. Add ribs, coating well. Cover bowl and marinate in the refrigerator for 24 to 48 hours. Drain ribs, reserving marinade. Grill ribs for approximately 20 minutes over medium-hot coals, turning and basting with reserved marinade about every 5 minutes. The ribs are done when they are cooked through and crispy on the outside.

Polly Perkins' Beef Tongue

SERVES 8

Long, gentle simmering tenderizes beef tongue (which can be tough if under cooked), and allowing it to cool in its cooking broth gives it added flavor. Serve it sliced with mustard or the sauce you like best.

1 smoked beef tongue, 2½ to 3 pounds
1 tablespoon salt
1 rib celery
1 whole clove
1 bay leaf
6 whole peppercorns
3 onions, chopped
1 clove garlic
¼ cup butter
1 cup dry white wine
1 cup water

Place tongue in a medium kettle and cover with cold water. Add salt, celery, clove, bay leaf, peppercorns, onion, and garlic. Bring to a boil, cover, reduce heat, and simmer for 3 hours. Remove tongue from water and cool. Peel tongue and remove bones and gristle from thick end and discard. Melt butter in deep pot and brown cleaned tongue all over. Add wine and cup of water and simmer 2 hours, turning after 1 hour. Remove from heat and cool in broth.

Sausage Casserole

SERVES 12

A perfect dish for lunch on a Sunday.

3 pounds bulk sausage
3 large stalks celery, chopped
3 bell peppers, chopped
2 medium onions, chopped
6 cups water
2 packages (4.5 ounces total) Lipton® chicken-noodle soup mix
1 10¾ can condensed cream of chicken soup
1½ cups uncooked rice
3 tablespoons soy sauce
1 4-ounce package slivered almonds

Fry sausage in a large pan until browned and cooked through. Remove sausage with a slotted spoon and crumble when cooled. Set sausage aside. Sauté celery, peppers, and onions in pan with the sausage juices until they are soft and lightly browned; set aside. In a large pot, bring water to a boil; add soup mix and rice, reduce to a slow simmer, and cook, uncovered, until rice is done and liquid has reduced. Remove soup mixture from the heat and mix in sausage, sautéed vegetables, cream of chicken soup, and soy sauce. Pour into 2 9x13-inch pans and top each with almonds. Bake in a preheated 350-degree oven, uncovered, for 30 minutes.

Sausage Stroganoff

SERVES 6

This version of beef Stroganoff made with sausage is made richer with sour cream just before serving. Make sure you heat the dish very carefully after adding the cream or it may separate on you—
not the worst thing in the world, but it doesn't make the dish that appetizing.

1 pound ground sausage, browned
½ cup minced onion
1 clove garlic, minced
¼ cup butter
2 tablespoons flour
2 teaspoons salt
¼ teaspoon black pepper
1 4-ounce can sliced mushrooms
1 10¾–ounce can condensed cream of chicken soup
1 cup sour cream

In a large skillet set over medium heat, cook the onions and garlic in the butter until they are tender. Stir in flour, salt, pepper, and mushrooms. Cook 5 minutes. Stir in soup. Lower heat and simmer, uncovered, 10 minutes. Stir in the browned sausage, then the sour cream and mix well. Heat the mixture through but do not let it boil. Serve over noodles.

Smithfield Ham Junior-Style

SERVES 8

For an extra-special touch, make a glaze by mixing together 1 can of cranberry sauce with ½ cup brown sugar; brush this on the ham while it's baking.

1 16- to 18-pound Smithfield ham
2 2-litre bottles Coca-Cola®
2 onions, sliced
½ cup vinegar
½ cup sugar
2 tablespoons dry mustard
whole cloves
1 cup brown sugar
maraschino cherries
canned pineapple slices

Soak ham in water for 10 to 12 hours and then scrub it well with a clean brush. Place ham in a large kettle and pour in the Coca-Cola, adding enough water to cover ham. Add onions, vinegar, sugar, and mustard. Bring to a boil on the stove, then reduce heat so it cooks at a low simmer. Simmer, uncovered, for 25 minutes per pound. Let ham cool in liquid for 2 to 3 hours and then discard the liquid.

Preheat oven to 300 degrees. Remove ham skin and stick a bunch of cloves in the top of the ham and sprinkle with brown sugar. Place ham in a large roasting pan fitted with a rack and bake for 1½ hours on low heat, or until a meat thermometer reads 180 degrees. Remove from the oven; decorate ham with cherries and pineapple slices before serving.

Stuffed Pork Chops

SERVES 6

A tasty spinach mixture fills the pockets cut in these pork chops. You can cut the pockets yourself with a sharp, thin-bladed knife (just be careful to make the opening as small as possible and do it carefully so you don't pierce the sides of the chops), but your butcher can also do it for you.

6 pork chops, approximately 1¼ inches thick
1 package (10 ounces) frozen chopped spinach
½ cup chopped onion
¾ cup chopped mushrooms
2 tablespoons oleo
1 teaspoon salt
¼ teaspoon nutmeg
⅛ teaspoon black pepper
1 14-ounce can chicken broth

Have butcher cut pockets in pork chops. Preheat oven to 325 degrees. Thaw and drain spinach and place it into a medium bowl. Sauté onion and mushrooms in oleo until cooked through and add them to the spinach. Add all remaining ingredients except broth and mix well. Fill pockets of chops with spinach mixture, place them in a shallow oven-proof glass pan and bake, uncovered, for 1 hour, basting with chicken broth and turning the pork chops every 10 minutes.

Suki-Aki

SERVES 4

Frozen green beans and broccoli work well in this recipe, but you can substitute frozen snow peas, carrots, or mixed oriental-style vegetables for them if you like.

1 pound pork or beef, cut into 1-inch cubes
3 tablespoons Crisco® or vegetable oil
2 teaspoons sugar
½ cup soy sauce
2 bunches green onions (scallions), sliced
1 cup celery, cut in strips
1 package mushrooms, cut up
1 9-ounce package frozen French-cut green beans, thawed
1 10-ounce package frozen broccoli, thawed

In a large pot or deep skillet, brown meat in fat over medium-high heat. Add soy sauce and sugar. Add onions, celery, and mushrooms and fry for 5 minutes. Add remaining vegetables and cook until tender. Serve over white rice.

Virginia Corn Scrapple

SERVES 8

This recipe calls for cooking your scrapple on top of the stove for a very long time. Make sure you check it often and stir it occasionally so that it doesn't stick or burn; adjust your heat if it does.

2 large onions, chopped
½ tablespoon butter
½ tablespoon lard
2 pounds ground round
1 cup cornmeal
1 28-ounce can crushed tomatoes
1 4-ounce can mushrooms
1 teaspoon salt
black pepper to taste

In a large skillet, brown onion in butter and lard. Stir in meat, then cornmeal, tomatoes, mushrooms, salt, and pepper to taste. Cook, uncovered, for 2 hours over low heat.

Chicken and Game Birds

There's more than one way to cook a goose but there's a heck of a lot more ways to cook a chicken.

Chicken is about the most versatile bird you can imagine, and we got a lot of imaginative ways to serve it up. Mostly you want to cook your poultry thoroughly, so it's safe and no one gets sick. But you just got to make sure it don't dry out and go all tasteless on you in the process. And we got a lot of interesting methods and some real good sauces to do just that. Now some folks insist that a farm-raised chicken has a flavor you just can't get from your commercial store-bought variety, and there's truth to that. If you can get free-range chickens then by all means use them. But we always get good results even from the ones at the supermarket, so don't worry yourself too much about it. If you've got a hunter in the family then you can get a whole lot of different birds that cook up real tasty, and there's a few recipes in this chapter for them as well.

Barbecued Chicken in a Paper Bag

SERVES 4

Believe me, folks, there is a method to the madness: The paper bag holds in all the steam and keeps this chicken very moist.

FOR THE BARBECUE SAUCE

3 tablespoons ketchup
2 tablespoons vinegar
2 tablespoons Worcestershire sauce
1 tablespoon lemon juice
¼ cup water
2 tablespoons butter
3 tablespoons brown sugar
1 teaspoon salt
1 teaspoon dry mustard
1 teaspoon chili powder
½ teaspoon cayenne
1 teaspoon paprika

FOR THE CHICKEN

1 3-pound chicken
salt and black pepper
1 medium-size heavy paper sack

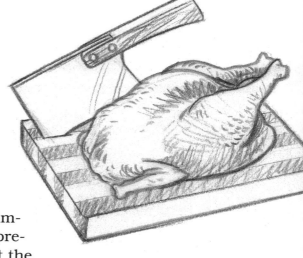

To make the sauce, mix all ingredients together in a saucepan and bring to a boil. Lower heat to medium-low and simmer for 10 minutes. Meanwhile, preheat the oven to 500 degrees. Cut the chicken into eight serving pieces and salt and pepper the pieces. Grease the inside of the paper sack and place it in a roaster. Dip each piece of chicken in the prepared sauce and place it in the sack along with any remaining sauce. Fold sack so it doesn't leak. Cover the roaster and bake in preheated oven for 15 minutes; lower heat to 350 degrees and bake an additional 1¼ hours. Do not open sack until it is finished cooking.

Chicken à la King

SERVES 6

Serve this on rice or in pastry shells.

5 whole chicken breasts, bone in
3 tablespoons butter
½ cup minced green bell pepper
1 4-ounce can sliced mushrooms, drained
3 tablespoons flour
1½ cups heavy cream
2 egg yolks, beaten
1 6½-ounce can pimientos, drained and chopped fine
salt and black pepper

Put chicken breasts in a large kettle and throw in whatever stock vegetables or flavorings you have around (a carrot or two, some onion, celery, parsley, a bay leaf, and a few whole peppercorns). Cover with cold water and bring to a boil. Lower heat and simmer, uncovered, until chicken is tender and cooked through, about an hour. Remove chicken breasts and allow them to cool. Strain the broth, discarding vegetables and spices, and set aside. When the chicken is cool, pick the meat off the bone and cut it into cubes. Over medium heat, melt butter in a skillet; add green pepper and mushrooms, and cook until the green pepper is tender. Add flour and stir until it is all smooth. Slowly add the broth you saved back into the skillet, whisking until smooth. Add in the cream. Stir this a lot until it thickens and comes to a boil. Get it off the heat and whisk in egg yolks. Stir in the cubed chicken and pimiento and add some salt and black pepper. Return the skillet to the heat and cook for a minute longer (but don't let it boil again).

Chicken International

SERVES 6

Sorta fancy but really good!

6 boneless, skinless half chicken breasts
½ stick (¼ cup) butter
1 14-ounce can chicken broth
½ teaspoon curry powder
½ onion, chopped
1 teaspoon salt
⅛ teaspoon black pepper
3 teaspoon cornstarch
1 6-ounce can mandarin orange sections, drained and juice reserved
1 teaspoon lemon juice
1 green bell pepper, thinly sliced
⅓ cup dates, pitted and chopped

In a large skillet, sauté chicken in butter over medium-high heat until browned. In a small bowl, combine chicken broth, curry powder, onion, salt, and black pepper; pour over chicken. Cover skillet, reduce heat, and simmer 45 minutes. Remove chicken pieces and keep them warm. Dissolve cornstarch in the juice from the mandarin oranges and add this and lemon juice to the skillet. Stir and cook until thickened. Add green pepper and dates and cook 5 minutes more. Gently stir in orange slices and pour sauce over chicken.

Chicken Loaf

SERVES 6

Topping this casserole with crushed potato chips adds a terrific contrast in texture, and the kids love it.

4 cups potato chips, crushed
4 cups diced cooked chicken
1 10¾-ounce can condensed cream of chicken soup
1 10¾-ounce can condensed cream of celery soup
1 6½-ounce can chopped pimientos, drained and chopped
¾ cup diced celery
¾ cup Miracle Whip®
¼ cup finely chopped onion
2 tablespoons lemon juice
6 hard-boiled eggs, chopped

Preheat the oven to 400 degrees. Grease a 9x13-inch baking pan and cover the bottom with half of the crushed potato chips. In a large bowl, thoroughly mix all the remaining ingredients except for the chopped egg and remaining chips. Fold in the chopped egg and pour the mixture over the chips in the pan. Top with the rest of the chips and bake for 30 to 40 minutes or until hot and bubbly.

Cornish Hens à la Dutch Oven

These small birds tenderize quickly, so watch them closely while they bake to avoid overcooking them.

6 Cornish hens
2 sticks (1 cup) butter
salt and black pepper
10 green onions (scallions), chopped
1 ½ 4-ounce cans mushrooms, drained
4 tablespoons chopped fresh parsley
1 cup sherry
½ cup water

Preheat oven to 300 degrees. Melt butter in a large Dutch oven. Salt and pepper hens and brown them in the butter over medium-high heat. Add remaining ingredients, cover, and bake in preheated oven for about 45 minutes. Watch them closely and baste them often. (You may prepare them ahead of time and reheat to serve, adding more butter, water, and sherry if you need it.) Place the hens on a serving platter and spoon sauce over them. Serve remaining sauce on the side.

Dixie Grilled Chicken

SERVES 6

The peanut butter adds an interesting twist to this chicken and helps to create beautiful grill marks on the chicken as the sugar in the peanut butter starts to caramelize.

6 chicken breasts, halved
salt and black pepper
Crisco® oil
2 tablespoons butter

1 tablespoon black pepper
2½ cups vinegar
1 tablespoon chili powder
2 tablespoons chunky peanut butter
2 teaspoons celery seed
2 tablespoons salt
½ cup lemon juice (bottled is fine)

Fix your grill. Sprinkle chicken with salt and pepper and rub with Crisco oil. In a saucepan, combine remaining ingredients and heat thoroughly. When coal bed is ready, place chicken on grill. Baste with sauce and turn frequently for 1½ hours, or until cooked through. It may take less time on your grill.

Down-Home Chicken Shortcake

SERVES AS MANY AS YOU LIKE

A lovely luncheon dish.

corn bread
sliced ham
sliced chicken
1 4-ounce can mushrooms
butter
thick cream sauce
sherry
Parmesan cheese
parsley sprigs and tomato wedges for garnish

Split and butter one 4-inch square of crisp brown corn bread for each serving. Lay a thin slice of ham and chicken on top of each half slice of corn bread. Sauté mushrooms in butter and add them to the thick cream sauce and flavor it with sherry. Pour an ample amount of sauce on each serving. Sprinkle with Parmesan cheese and brown slightly under the broiler. Garnish each serving with a parsley sprig and a tomato wedge.

Dove Pie

SERVES 3

Doves are perfect for this cooking method, which leaves their meat tender and mild. If you're not lucky enough to have a hunter in the family, you can substitute quail from your butcher for the doves in this pie.

6 doves
½ cup flour
1 teaspoon salt
¼ teaspoon black pepper
¾ stick (6 tablespoons) butter
1 tablespoon salad oil
¼ cup minced onions
¼ cup chopped green bell pepper
1 cup water
1 cup dry red wine
1 cup Worcestershire sauce
2 hard-boiled eggs
pie crust

Catch, kill, draw, singe, and wash your doves. Mix flour, salt, and pepper in a paper bag. Drop doves in the bag and shake it up hard so you coat those doves. Melt butter and oil in a skillet and brown doves well on all sides. Remove doves and add onion and green pepper to skillet and cook for 5 minutes. Put doves back in skillet and add water, wine, and Worcestershire. Cover and simmer for 1 hour or until doves are tender.

Preheat oven to 400 degrees. Place doves and gravy in a 3-quart casserole and slice eggs over top. Cover with pie crust, pressing the crust firmly to the top of the casserole. Make 3 slits in top of crust. Bake in preheated oven for 12 minutes, or until crust is golden brown. Serve right out of the oven.

Hot Chicken Salad Casserole

SERVES 8

This casserole is similar to the Chicken Loaf recipe (see page 57), with the addition of almonds and cooked rice.

¾ cup Hellmann's® mayonnaise
¼ cup water
1 10¾-ounce can condensed cream of chicken soup
2 cups diced cooked chicken
2 tablespoons grated onion
½ cup chopped almonds
¼ cup diced green bell pepper
1½ cups cooked rice
½ teaspoon salt
3 hard-boiled eggs, sliced
2 cups crushed potato chips

Preheat oven to 350 degrees. Mix mayonnaise, water, and soup together. Stir in chicken, onion, almonds, green pepper, rice, and salt. Carefully add sliced eggs. Place all in a greased casserole, top with potato chips, and bake uncovered for 30 minutes or until bubbling and browned.

Wild Turkey

SERVES 6

Roasting wild turkey under a "slop cloth" dipped in bacon keeps the bird tender and moist.

1 wild turkey, 8 to 10 pounds
bacon fat
salt and black pepper
1 cup chopped onion
2 cups chopped celery
1½ cups white wine
1 muslin cloth

Catch, kill, draw, singe, and wash wild turkey. Preheat oven to 300 degrees. Dry the turkey well, rub it down with bacon fat, and sprinkle it with salt and pepper. Fill cavity of bird with onion, celery, and 1 cup of the white wine. Truss the bird and place it in a shallow roasting pan. Dip muslin cloth in more bacon fat and cover turkey with this slop cloth. Place the turkey in the oven and roast for 3 hours or more, or until a thermometer inserted in the thigh of the bird reads 195 degrees. While it's roasting, baste it several times with remaining ½ cup white wine and pan drippings. Discard stuffing and serve.

Fish and Seafood

If we were highfalutin rich folk, I guess Junior would take up golf. As it is, he just goes fishing. In my mind, golfing and fishing are just about the same thing: real good wastes of time. True, you don't get to eat the golf ball, but you don't have to scale it and gut it either.

If you've got fresh fish around we think there's not much else better, but if you don't, don't let that stop you—it sure doesn't stop us in these parts. Frozen fish works well most of the time, and even canned clams and tuna fish have their place in some really special dishes. But going back to fresh seafood, shrimp is real popular, both deep-fried or cooked up in stews, so you'll find a few recipes for that, too. Now there are a lot of folks that will tell you you can't be too careful about not overcooking your fish, and there are even some who eat seafood raw, but that's not our style. You'll see that when we cook fish, we really cook it, we just use a number of techniques and sauces to make sure it don't get dried out and tasteless.

Barbecued Fish Trout

SERVES 2

A real nice way to cook not just trout but any kind of whole fish and a good recipe for picnics, camping trips, and other backyard activities.

2 trout, scaled and gutted
salt and black pepper
1 stick (½ cup) butter, melted
3 tablespoons grated onion
juice of 2 lemons
2 tablespoons chopped fresh parsley
2 tablespoons Worcestershire sauce
2 dashes Tabasco®

Fix your grill. Salt and pepper the trout and place them on a sheet of heavy-duty foil. Combine remaining ingredients and pour over fish. Seal foil, making sure there are no leaks. When the coal bed is ready, place foil packet on the grill and cook for 1½ hours, turning the packets every 30 minutes. Remove fish from foil and place them on the grill for an additional 10 minutes on each side, basting them with the sauce.

Creamy Clam Spaghetti

SERVES 8

This version of spaghetti with white clam sauce gets its richness from heavy cream.

4 6½-ounce cans minced clams
2 sticks (1 cup) butter
6 cloves garlic, minced
juice of ½ lemon
1 tablespoon grated onion
¼ teaspoon white pepper
¼ cup fresh parsley, chopped
2 tablespoons cornstarch
½ pint (1 cup) heavy cream
2 pounds spaghetti

Drain clams, reserving juice, and set clams aside. Combine clam juice, butter, garlic, lemon juice, onion, white pepper, and parsley in a saucepan and simmer for 15 minutes. Dissolve cornstarch in cream and stir it into the butter mixture along with the clams. Cook, stirring often, for an additional 15 minutes. Meanwhile, prepare 2 pounds spaghetti according to package directions. Pour sauce over hot noodles, toss, and serve.

Catch of the Day

SERVES 4

This is about the simplest dish you can imagine. It works just as well with any other kind of fillets, even fresh ones.

2 pounds frozen flounder fillets, thawed
½ cup mayonnaise
½ teaspoon dried parsley
½ teaspoon dried chives

Preheat oven to 400 degrees. Place fish in a greased 9-inch-square glass baking dish. Spread with mayonnaise and sprinkle with parsley and chives. Cover with foil and bake 30 minutes, until fish is easily flaked with a fork.

Escalloped Oysters

SERVES 6 TO 8

Shucking raw oysters can be pretty frustrating if you're not practiced at it. If you're not up for it your fish seller can do it for you, or you may be able to buy oysters already shucked in your grocery store. Anyway you choose, be sure to save as much of the oysters' "liquor" (liquid) as possible for this casserole.

1 quart oysters, picked clean, with their liquor
3 tablespoons butter, plus a little more for buttering the casserole
salt and black pepper to taste
2 cups oyster crackers
1 egg
½ cup milk
½ cup bread crumbs

Preheat oven to 375 degrees. In a small saucepan set over low heat, warm the oysters in their own liquid until they are just lukewarm; drain and save juice. Butter a 2-quart casserole. Make layers of oysters, salt and pepper, crackers, and small bits of butter. Continue making layers until all oysters are used. Whisk the egg into the milk and whisk in the oyster juice; pour over the oysters, letting the crackers absorb the liquid. Top the casserole with bread crumbs and bake in preheated oven for 30 to 40 minutes.

Fish Pudding

SERVES 4

This baked pudding is a good way to use up leftover fish. You can certainly increase the amount of fish called for if you have more around.

1 cup cooked, shredded fish
1 cup cracker crumbs
¾ cup milk
¾ cup whipping cream
1 teaspoon salt
2 tablespoons minced fresh parsley
1 stick (½ cup) butter, melted
3 egg whites

Preheat oven to 325 degrees. Mix together fish, cracker crumbs, milk, cream, and salt. Let stand 5 minutes. Add parsley and melted butter. Whip egg whites until stiff but not dry and fold them into the fish mixture. Pour into a greased casserole and bake for 35 minutes, or until lightly browned and bubbly. Serve with tartar sauce.

Plantation Fried Shrimp

SERVES 6

The secrets to deep-fried shrimp are: to have your oil hot enough (350 to 375 degrees—a small piece of bread dropped into the oil should sink briefly and then rise to the top and begin bubbling rapidly); to fry them in batches to avoid overcrowding your fryer; and serve them as quickly as possible once they're fried.

2 pounds raw shrimp in the shell
2 eggs
2 tablespoons milk
cracker crumbs
salt and black pepper to taste
Mazola® oil for deep frying

Peel shrimp, leaving the tail section intact (you can also devein them if you want). In a small bowl, whisk together eggs and milk and set aside. Put cracker crumbs and salt and pepper on a plate and mix well. Dip shrimp in the egg mixture and then roll them in the crackers crumbs. Fry shrimp in hot oil until golden brown, about 5 minutes. Drain on paper towels. Serve hot.

Shrimp Creole

SERVES 6

Increase the amount of Tabasco in this recipe if you want it spicier, or just put the bottle on the the table so your guests can make theirs as hot as they like.

2 tablespoons butter
1 large onion, chopped
2 stalks celery, chopped
1 tablespoon flour
1 28-ounce can crushed tomatoes

salt and black pepper to taste
2 pounds raw shrimp, peeled
4 drops Tabasco®
1 teaspoon cornstarch

In a heavy pot melt butter; add onion and celery and cook until they become transparent. Mix in flour and cook, stirring, for 2 minutes. Add tomatoes, salt and pepper, shrimp, Tabasco, and enough water to sauce. Cook gently, uncovered, for 20 minutes. Just before serving, add cornstarch to thicken sauce. Serve over white rice.

Trout Florentine

SERVES 4

This recipe calls for canned hollandaise. If your grocery store doesn't stock this you can use one of those dried mixes or make your own from scratch.

2 12-ounce packages Stouffer's® spinach soufflé
4 trout, filleted
water
½ cup white wine
1 can hollandaise sauce

Cook spinach soufflé according to package directions. When soufflé is within 20 minutes of being done, place trout in a shallow baking dish. Surround fish with water, but do not cover, and add wine. Poach fillets until meat is opaque (you can do this either on top of the stove at a bare simmer, or in the oven with the soufflé). Discard the poaching liquid and place fish fillets on plate, spoon spinach soufflé over fillets, and top with warm hollandaise.

Vesta's Tuna-Noodle Casserole

SERVES 6

This is one fish dish that even seafood haters seem to love.

1 6-ounce package medium egg noodles
1 6-ounce can tuna, drained
½ cup mayonnaise
1 cup sliced celery
⅓ cup diced onion
¼ cup chopped pimiento
1 teaspoon salt
1 10¾-ounce can condensed cream of celery soup
½ cup milk
4 ounces (1 cup) shredded cheddar cheese
½ cup slivered almonds

Preheat oven to 425 degrees. Cook noodles according to package directions and drain. Combine noodles, tuna, mayonnaise, celery, onion, pimiento, and salt and set aside. Blend soup and milk, beating thoroughly. Add cheese and heat, stirring, until cheese melts. Combine soup with noodle mixture and pour into an ungreased 2-quart casserole. Sprinkle with almonds. Bake 20 to 30 minutes, until bubbly.

Vegetables and Salads

Down South they got this trick for making vegetables taste like they're not vegetables. Well, that's fine if you don't like vegetables, but here's even better news: If you enjoy limas, corn, and greens, like we do around here, these vegetables taste terrific, and still taste like vegetables.

Don't worry if you don't have a lot of fresh vegetables around, either. A lot of recipes below use frozen and canned vegetables dressed up with any number of ingredients—cheese, sour cream, Tabasco, and, of course, condensed soups—to make them real special. A number are practically staples for picnics and big parties, among them Baked Beans and Ham, Nine-Day Slaw, and Olé Mexican Salad, so be sure to give one a try at your next to-do.

Baked Beans and Ham

SERVES 25

Around here we get real patriotic with this one—it is a Fourth of July picnic favorite.

1 stick (½ cup) butter
½ pound ground chuck
½ pound ham, ground
1 rib celery, chopped
3 onions, chopped
1 teaspoon salt
10 cups pork and beans
1 small can (6½ ounces) chopped pimientos
1 12-ounce bottle ketchup
1 4-ounce can sliced mushrooms, drained
2 tablespoons brown sugar
¼ pound (1 cup) grated cheese (use your favorite)

Combine butter, ground chuck, ham, celery, and onions in a skillet and sauté for 30 minutes. Add all remaining ingredients except cheese and stir. Pour into a casserole, top with the cheese, and bake in a preheated 350-degree oven for 45 minutes.

Beer-Batter Vegetables

MAKES AS MUCH AS YOU LIKE

This is the only way I can get my kids to eat vegetables.

**any or all of the following vegetables: broccoli, cauliflower, whole mush-
rooms, squash, sweet potatoes, onions**
peanut oil
flour
beer
salt
ranch dressing for dipping

Break up the cauliflower and broccoli into bite-size florets. Slice
squash and sweet potatoes ⅛ inch thick. Slice the onions a bit thicker and separate into rings. In a chicken fryer, heat peanut oil
(knuckle-high's worth). While that's heating up, whisk flour, beer, and
salt together until it's smooth and you've got a consistency about like
pancake batter. When oil is hot, dip each vegetable into batter and fry
until golden brown. Drain on paper towels and serve immediately with
ranch dressing for dipping.

Broccoli Rice Surprise

SERVES 6

Frozen green beans or spinach can be substituted for the broccoli.

2 cups cooked rice
1 10-ounce package frozen chopped broccoli, cooked and drained
1 8-ounce jar Cheez Whiz®
1 10¾-ounce can condensed cream of chicken soup
1 8-ounce can water chestnuts, drained and chopped

Preheat oven to 350 degrees. Mix together rice, broccoli, and Cheez
Whiz. Fold in soup and water chestnuts. Bake for 30 minutes, uncovered, until bubbly.

Cabbage with Beer and Bouillon

SERVES 6

Using a pressure cooker makes this dish a snap. If you don't have one, cook it on top of the stove over medium heat, covered, stirring occasionally until the cabbage is tender—it will take you a lot longer, that's all.

1½ pounds cabbage, shredded
2 cups chicken bouillon
1 cup beer
½ teaspoon black pepper
grated Parmesan cheese

Combine cabbage, bouillon, beer, and pepper in a pressure cooker. Cover securely and cook at 15 pounds pressure for 5 minutes. Cool pressure cooker at once under cold water. Drain cabbage, garnish with Parmesan cheese, and serve.

Corn Fritters

SERVES 6

Fritters are a popular side dish around here, and these are about as simple to prepare as they get. Bacon grease is the fat of choice to fry them with, but any oil will do the trick.

1 cup milk
1 egg
1 tablespoon flour
1 10-ounce package frozen corn, thawed
1 tablespoon baking powder
½ teaspoon salt

Mix milk, egg, and flour together. Add remaining ingredients. Drop by tablespoonfuls on a hot griddle coated with bacon grease. Fry until the fritters are browned.

Frito Tomatoes

SERVES 6

Vary the amount of Tabasco used in this recipe to suit your taste, or omit it all together if your taste buds are delicate.

3 tablespoons butter
1 large onion, diced
1 green bell pepper, diced
2 cloves garlic, minced
1 to 2 cans (14.5 ounces each) chopped tomatoes
1 4¼-ounce package Fritos®
1 teaspoon Worcestershire sauce
Tabasco® to taste
1½ cups shredded cheddar cheese

Preheat oven to 350 degrees. Melt butter and cook up onion, green pepper, and garlic until soft. Add tomatoes, Worcestershire, and Tabasco and cook over medium heat for 3 minutes. Remove pan from the heat and add Fritos and 1 cup of the cheese and let Fritos absorb liquid. Place into a casserole dish and top with remaining ½ cup cheese. Bake until cheese melts.

Fried Corn

SERVES 4

Try this home-made version of creamed corn—believe it or not it sure beats the stuff in cans!

**6 to 8 medium ears of corn or 1 large package
frozen corn, thawed and drained.
½ cup bacon drippings
1 cup coffee cream (half-and-half)
salt and black pepper to taste**

Cut kernels from the cob and scrape the cob to remove all the milk. Have a skillet very hot and add bacon drippings and corn. Stir constantly until the corn just begins to brown, about 5 minutes. Add the cream and season with salt and pepper. Cover and simmer for 15 minutes or until thick.

Frozen Pineapple Salad

SERVES 8

This is a popular alternative to your standard salad and should please anyone who thinks of greens as "rabbit food."

**1 pint (2 cups) sour cream
2 tablespoons lemon juice
¾ cup sugar
1 8-ounce can crushed pineapple, with liquid
½ cup chopped maraschino cherries
¼ cup pecan pieces
2 bananas, peeled and sliced
½ cup mini-marshmallows**

Mix sour cream, lemon juice, and sugar. Add remaining ingredients and mix well. Pour into a mold sprayed with Pam and freeze until firm, 8 hours or overnight. Unmold the salad and slice.

Green Bean Casserole

SERVES 10

Well worth the effort!

1 pound fresh mushrooms, sliced
1 medium onion, chopped
1 stick (½ cup) butter
¼ cup flour
2 cups warm milk
1 cup coffee cream (half-and-half)
¾ pound sharp cheddar cheese, grated
¼ teaspoon Tabasco®
2 teaspoons soy sauce
1 teaspoon salt
¼ teaspoon black pepper
1 teaspoon Ac'cent®
3 9-ounce packages frozen cut green beans
1 8-ounce can water chestnuts, drained and sliced
¾ cup slivered almonds

Preheat oven to 375 degrees. Sauté mushrooms and onion in butter. Add flour and stir until smooth. Add warm milk and coffee cream. Put mixture in the top of a double boiler set over boiling water and cook until it thickens. Add cheese, Tabasco, soy sauce, salt, pepper, and Ac'cent and cook until cheese melts. Cook beans until just tender, drain, and mix into the sauce along with the water chestnuts. Pour mixture into a 3-quart casserole, top with almonds, and bake for 20 minutes or until bubbling and lightly browned.

Ham Hocks and Greens

SERVES 8

Serve this with corn bread, sliced tomatoes, and sliced sweet onion.

3½ pounds ham hocks
3 tablespoons vegetable oil
4 cups water
1 large onion, chopped
1 pound mustard greens, washed and drained
½ pound turnip greens
½ pound collard greens

In a large pot, brown ham hocks in oil. Add water and onion and bring to a boil. Add greens and bring to boil again. Reduce heat, cover, and simmer 1½ to 2 hours. Drain, remove ham hocks, and cut meat into bite-size pieces. Add meat to greens.

Nine-Day Slaw

SERVES 8 TO 10

Make this slaw up a day in advance if you can so that the cabbage softens and the flavors develop.

1 medium cabbage, shredded
2 stalks celery, sliced
2 medium onions, diced
1 green bell pepper, diced
2 cups plus 2 tablespoons sugar
1 cup salad oil
1 cup cider vinegar
2 tablespoons salt
1 small can (6½ ounces) pimientos, chopped and drained

Combine cabbage, celery, onion, and green pepper. Add 2 cups of the sugar and blend well. In a saucepan, combine oil, vinegar, salt, and remaining 2 tablespoons of sugar and bring to a boil, stirring constantly. Pour hot dressing over cabbage mixture and allow to cool. Gently fold in pimientos. Cover and store in the icebox for 24 hours before serving.

Nutty Broccoli

SERVES 6

Broccoli, cashews, and sour cream make this a rich and delicious side. You could substitute fresh broccoli florets for the frozen variety, but only if you care for the extra work of washing and trimming.

2 tablespoons minced onion
2 tablespoons butter
1 cup sour cream
2 teaspoons sugar
1 teaspoon white vinegar
½ teaspoon poppy seeds
½ teaspoon paprika
dash of salt
2 10-ounce packages frozen broccoli, cooked and drained
1 4-ounce package cashew nuts, chopped

Cook onion in butter until clear. Remove from heat and stir in sour cream, sugar, vinegar, poppy seeds, paprika, and salt. Pour over cooked, drained broccoli. Sprinkle chopped cashew nuts on top and serve.

Olé Mexican Salad

SERVES 20

Avocados discolor quickly when sliced, so this recipe calls for dipping them in lemon juice (bottled is fine) to keep them pretty and green.

FOR THE DRESSING

2 8-ounce cartons sour cream
1 small bottle (8 ounces) Wish-Bone® Italian dressing
3 tablespoons chili powder
garlic salt to taste

FOR THE SALAD

10 avocados, peeled, sliced, and slices dipped in lemon juice
1 package cherry tomatoes
5 15-ounce cans kidney beans (drained and rinsed)
2 or 3 heads lettuce, shredded
1 large package Fritos®, crushed

To make the dressing, place sour cream, Wish-Bone dressing, and chili powder in a bowl and mix well. Season with garlic salt.

To make the salad, marinate sliced avocados, tomatoes, and kidney beans in dressing mixture for several hours. Before serving, add lettuce and Fritos and mix well to combine.

Quick Asparagus Soufflé

SERVES 4

One of the tricks to getting a good, light soufflé is whipping your egg whites until they're just stiff but not dry.

1 10¾-ounce can cream of asparagus soup
1 cup finely grated cheddar cheese

4 eggs, separated
dash Tabasco®
1 teaspoon Worcestershire sauce

Preheat oven to 425 degrees. In a saucepan, cook soup and cheese over low heat until cheese is melted. Lightly beat egg yolks and add them slowly to the soup, stirring constantly. Add Tabasco and Worcestershire. Remove from heat and let cool slightly. Beat egg whites until they hold stiff peaks and gently fold them into the asparagus mixture. Pour into a greased casserole and bake for 25 minutes.

7-Up Salad

SERVES 4 TO 6

Unmold this salad on a platter lined with iceberg lettuce leaves.

1 3-ounce package lemon Jell-O®
1 cup hot water
8 ounces cream cheese, softened
1 8-ounce can crushed pineapple, drained
1 4-ounce can chopped pecans
1 can (12 ounces) 7-Up®

Dissolve Jell-O in hot water and let it cool. Beat in cream cheese; add pineapple, nuts, and 7-Up. Pour into a greased mold and let sit in the icebox overnight. Unmold before serving.

Sunday Lima Bean Casserole

SERVES 8

This can be made ahead and reheated.

1 stick (½ cup) butter
1 cup flour
4 cups milk
3 or 4 shakes Worcestershire sauce
½ cup Durkee® dressing
1 cup grated sharp cheddar cheese
1½ pounds fresh mushrooms, sliced
2 9-ounce packages frozen lima beans, cooked according to package directions
4 hard-boiled eggs, chopped
Tabasco® and salt to taste
buttered bread crumbs

Preheat oven to 350 degrees. Over medium heat, melt butter in a large saucepan and stir in flour; cook for 3 minutes stirring constantly (don't let it brown). Stir in milk and continue to cook until you have a thick cream sauce. Season generously with Worcestershire and Durkee dressing. Add cheese, mushrooms, lima beans, eggs, and Tabasco and salt. Pour into a casserole and cover with bread crumbs. Bake, uncovered, until crumbs are browned, about 30 minutes.

Tater Skins

SERVES 6 TO 12

Use the potato flesh you scoop out of the skins to make mashed potatoes.

12 small baking potatoes, scrubbed and rubbed with oil
2 sticks (1 cup) butter, melted
½ pound bacon, cooked and crumbled

12 ounces grated cheddar cheese
1 bunch green onions (scallions), chopped
1 8-ounce container sour cream

Preheat oven to 400 degrees. Bake the potatoes for 1 hour and remove from oven. Cut each potato in half the long way and let 'em cool. Scoop out the centers of the potatoes and brush the skins with butter. Lower oven temperature to 300 degrees and return the skins to the oven for 20 minutes. Sprinkle bacon and cheese over the inside of the skins and return them to the oven until the cheese is melted. Remove from the oven and garnish with green onions and sour cream.

Turnip Puff

SERVES 4 TO 6

If your turnips come with the green tops still on, be sure to save them and cook them down just like you would other greens, or use them in the recipe for Ham Hocks and Greens (see page 78).

1 pound turnips
2 tablespoons butter or oleo
2 lightly beaten eggs
¾ cup soft bread crumbs
1 tablespoon finely chopped onion
1 tablespoon snipped fresh parsley
1 tablespoon sugar
1 teaspoon lemon juice
salt to taste

Peel and cut turnips into ¾-inch cubes (you should have about 3 cups). Cook turnips, covered, in a small amount of boiling, salted water until tender, about 20 minutes. Drain, add butter, and mash. Meanwhile, in a bowl, combine eggs, bread crumbs, onion, parsley, sugar, and lemon juice. Add mashed turnips and mix well. Place this mixture into a small ungreased casserole and bake in a preheated 375-degree oven for 25 to 30 minutes or until hot.

Sandwiches

This is a true fact from history: There was this guy named Earl Sandwich and he just loved to go hunting. He would hunt all day long and never even take a break for lunch. Now his wife, Mrs. Sandwich, being the good responsible sort, was always trying to figure out ways of getting him to sit down and have a meal. She got to thinking about just putting some meat between two pieces of bread so Earl could eat and shoot at the same time. Now Earl was kind of forgetful and his hunting buddies were always chasing after him with things that he left behind. They'd be running after him hollering, "Hey Sandwich, Sandwich, here's that thing your wife cooked." The rest is history.

Just about no one gets tired of sandwiches, maybe because there's so much variety in what you can do with them. You can slap just about anything between two pieces of bread and chances are it'll be good, and you don't need a recipe for that. But in this chapter you'll find the ones that folks we know like best (and believe me, not all are to everyone's taste!). As to bread, we're not so picky about it as some might be; your favorite kind of bread will work just fine for any of these recipes.

Baby Sister's Favorite Sandwich

MAKES 1 SANDWICH

Some folks like potato chips with their sandwiches, but Baby Sister likes them in hers.

2 slices white bread
mayonnaise
potato chips

Spread mayonnaise on both pieces of bread. Pile potato chips on one piece. Serve the remaining piece of bread on the side so Baby Sister can smash it down.

Elvis Sandwich

MAKES 1 SANDWICH

The King made this one popular, but it isn't only just the rich-and-famous that likes it.

peanut butter
bananas
mayonnaise
2 slices white bread

In a bowl, mix peanut butter, bananas, and mayonnaise until thoroughly combined. Spread white bread with extra mayonnaise if you like.

Fried Bologna Sandwich

MAKES 1 SANDWICH

This is how I get Junior to eat lettuce.

bologna
butter
mayonnaise
2 slices white bread
lettuce

Fry bologna in a skillet with butter. Spread mayonnaise on bread and top with fried bologna and lettuce. You can melt cheese on this one if you like.

Fried Egg Sandwich

MAKES 1 SANDWICH

Don't think that this sandwich is just for breakfast—it hits the spot any time of day when you're up for something real tasty.

2 slices white bread, toasted
2 slices American cheese
mayonnaise
2 fried eggs

Melt cheese on toast; top with mayonnaise and fried eggs. Serve warm.

Grilled Cheese Surprise

MAKES 2 SANDWICHES

Kids love 'em!

4 slices bread
butter
mustard
8 slices American cheese
2 hot dogs, cooked
pickle relish

Butter one side of each piece of bread and lay the buttered side down on the counter. Put mustard on each side that is up, followed by 2 slices of cheese. Slice the cooked franks into rounds and place the slices on two of the pieces of bread. Sprinkle the franks with relish and cover with the remaining slices of bread, cheese-side down. Grill the buttered sides of the sandwiches on a lightly buttered griddle set over medium heat until the cheese is melted and the bread is toasted.

Leftover Chicken-Fried Steak Sandwich

MAKES 1 SANDWICH

Make sure you save the leftover gravy for this one.

Slices of bread
butter
Chicken-Fried Steak leftovers
leftover gravy
Miracle Whip® (optional)

Use a nice thick kind of bread and toast it with lots of butter, and I do mean lots. Stick your leftover chicken-fried steak in the microwave for a few seconds. Slap that and some cold gravy on the bread and honey, you won't know what hit you. If you really want to do something special, spread a layer of Miracle Whip on it.

Meat Loaf Sandwich

MAKES AS MANY AS YOU WANT TO

This is definitely one of my personal favorites.

white bread
Miracle Whip®
ketchup
leftover meat loaf
sweet pickle relish
thinly sliced onion

Spread Miracle Whip and ketchup on both pieces of white bread. Slap on meat loaf, pickle relish, and onion.

Sloppy Joe's

SERVES 6

Potato chips are the best side dish to serve with this easy, cheap version of Sloppy Joe's. The kids say they like these even better than the ones they get in the school cafeteria.

1 pound ground beef
1 small onion, chopped up
½ cup celery, chopped up
¼ cup green bell pepper, chopped up
1 carrot, grated
1 14-ounce bottle tomato ketchup
salt and black pepper to taste
6 sandwich rolls

Brown beef in a skillet. Stir in onion and celery and cook until brown. Add all the other ingredients except sandwich rolls and cook for an hour or so. Spoon mixture over sandwich rolls.

Truck Man's Sandwich

MAKES 1 SANDWICH

This is best when wrapped in a brown paper bag, left on the passenger seat, and warmed by the sun (just a little joke).

2 slices white bread
Miracle Whip®
leftover gravy
leftover turkey
leftover stuffing
leftover cranberry mold

Put lots of Miracle Whip on one side of a slice of bread. Spread the cold gravy generously on the other slice and pile everything else on. Make a bunch and give them to your kids and your man when they leave in the morning.

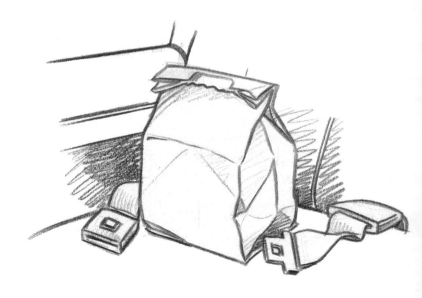

Breads

Look, you've got a leaky faucet and a plate full of gravy. If you're a fool, you'll ask Junior to fix the leak and you'll start scooping the gravy with a fork. Both jobs will never get done. Now, on the other hand, if you think about it, you'll call a plumber. You'll also pick up a hunk of bread and sop up that gravy the way it was meant to be eaten. You see, bread is like having your own personal plumber...only difference is that the loaf of bread doesn't overcharge so darn much.

The recipes included here will keep you eating bread throughout the week. Some are yeast-risen, which means they take a bit of doing on your part—but not too much, and they're worth the effort. Others are quick-rising breads, biscuits, and muffins that are a cinch to whip up at the last minute. And one recipe even uses the prepared ready-to-bake biscuits you can buy in the refrigerator section of your supermarket if you really don't feel like working in the kitchen. Unless specified otherwise, all the recipes here should be prepared with regular, all-purpose flour.

Bran Ice-Box Rolls

MAKES 24 ROLLS

The dough for these rolls will keep in your icebox for 2 to 3 days, so you can use it as needed.

1 cup boiling water
1 cup bran flakes
¾ cup shortening
¾ cup sugar
1 yeast cake (⅔ ounces), or 2 teaspoons dry yeast
1¼ teaspoons salt
2 eggs, beaten
1 cup warm water
5 cups flour

Pour boiling water over bran flakes. Add shortening and sugar. Cool. In another bowl, mix yeast, salt, eggs, and warm water together. Combine the two mixtures. Add 4 cups flour and stir well. Knead dough, using the remaining 1 cup flour to dust your work surface, for 5 to 10 minutes or until smooth and elastic. Put dough in a large greased bowl and set in the icebox. To make rolls, pinch off bits of dough, form them into balls, and let them rise in a greased pan at room temperature for about 2 hours. Bake in a preheated 375-degree oven for 20 minutes or until golden brown.

Carolyn's Rolls

MAKES 18 TO 20 ROLLS

I always put my bread dough on top of the icebox to rise so the draft don't catch it when Junior and the kids run in and out of the house.

1½ cups milk
2 packages dry yeast
½ cup lukewarm water
½ cup sugar
⅓ cup oil
1 tablespoon salt
2 eggs, lightly beaten
5½ cups flour

Scald the milk and set aside until lukewarm. In a large bowl, dissolve the yeast in the lukewarm water and add the sugar, oil, salt, eggs, and lukewarm milk and mix well. Stir in the flour, adding more if the dough seems too loose. Knead dough for approximately 5 minutes or until it is smooth and elastic. Put dough in a large greased bowl, cover with a dish towel, and let rise in a warm place until doubled in size. Roll out on floured board, cut with a biscuit cutter, and place on greased baking sheets. (The rolls may be dipped in melted butter before baking.) Bake in a preheated 400-degree oven for 10 to 15 minutes or until golden brown.

Cheese Biscuits

MAKES 10 BISCUITS

Cheddar cheese dresses up your store-bought biscuits in this simple recipe. You can substitute just about any other cheese you want for cheddar, but remember that American cheese can get a little rubbery when it's melted so you might want to use something else.

6 tablespoons oleo, melted
1 ten-biscuit tube ready-to-bake biscuits
1½ cups grated cheddar cheese

Pour melted oleo into an 8x8-inch baking pan. Place biscuits in pan and cover with grated cheddar cheese. Bake in preheated oven according to package directions.

Creamed Mexican Cornbread

SERVES 6

The heat of the jalapeños in this recipe will be balanced by the sour cream and creamed corn. But if you're afraid of the heat, use fewer peppers (or even leave them out altogether).

1 cup self-rising cornmeal
½ teaspoon salt
2 eggs
½ cup vegetable oil
1 8-ounce carton sour cream
1 8½-ounce can cream-style corn
2 to 4 jalapeño peppers, chopped
4 tablespoons chopped green bell peppers
4 tablespoons chopped onion
1 cup grated cheddar cheese

Preheat oven to 400 degrees. Grease a 9x13-inch baking pan. Combine first six ingredients, mixing well. Add remaining ingredients and stir to combine. Pour batter into prepared pan. Bake 25 to 30 minutes, or until the cornbread just begins to pull away from the sides of the pan.

Mama Earleen's Bread

SERVES 6 TO 8

The texture of this bread is similar to a firm corn pudding . . . talk about comfort food!

2 cups cooked grits, hot
3 tablespoons butter
4 eggs
2 cups milk
1 cup cornmeal
½ teaspoon salt

Preheat oven to 350 degrees. Mix hot cooked grits with butter. Beat eggs thoroughly and add to grits, stirring well after each addition. Stir in cornmeal and salt. (Batter should be the consistency of thick baked custard; add a little more milk if necessary.) Spoon batter into a deep, greased casserole dish and bake in preheated oven for 45 to 60 minutes, or until you see it begin to pull away from the sides of the pan.

Mush Hush Puppies

MAKES 6 DOZEN

Use peanut oil or vegetable oil, which ever you prefer, for frying these cornmeal hush puppies.

2 cups white cornmeal
2 cups flour
3 teaspoons baking powder
2 teaspoons salt
1 teaspoon pepper
1 medium onion, chopped
3 cups milk
fat for deep frying

Sift dry ingredients together; add onion. Add milk until the batter still holds its shape but is soft enough to slip easily off a spoon. Heat fat in a deep kettle. When very hot, drop batter by tablespoons into hot fat. Fry until lightly browned and transfer to paper towels to drain. Serve immediately.

Mush Muffins

MAKES 30 MUFFINS

A recipe for the men in your life. Remember to only try this recipe with old-fashioned, iron muffin tins.

1½ cups cornmeal
6 cups water
1 teaspoon salt
2 eggs
2 tablespoons shortening

Combine cornmeal, water, and salt and put in the top of a double boiler. Cook over simmering water until the mixture becomes the consistency of grits; remove from heat. Preheat oven to 450 degrees. Grease muffin irons thoroughly and heat in oven until hot, about 10 minutes. Meanwhile, beat eggs and shortening into the cornmeal mixture. Fill hot muffin irons ½ full with batter. Bake in preheated oven for 30 minutes, or until muffins are crisp on the outside but still mushy on the inside.

Never-Fail Biscuits

MAKES 16 TO 20 SMALL BISCUITS

The secret to great biscuits is not handling your dough too much, so don't worry if it's a bit lumpy.

2 cups flour
½ teaspoon salt
¼ teaspoon baking soda
2 teaspoon baking powder
¼ cup shortening
⅔ cup buttermilk

Preheat oven to 475 degrees. Sift dry ingredients. Cut in shortening with two knives. Stir in the buttermilk, handling the dough as little as possible. Roll dough out on a floured surface and cut biscuits out with a small biscuit cutter or the top of a small glass. Transfer biscuits to a greased baking sheet and bake in preheated oven for 10 to 15 minutes, or until lightly browned.

Poppy-Seed Turnovers

MAKES 4 LARGE OR 8 SMALL TURNOVERS

My 16-year-old baby-sitter loves these as much as the 6-year-old twins do!

¼ **cup minced onion**
1 **tablespoon shortening**
1 **pound ground beef**
½ **teaspoon salt**
⅛ **teaspoon black pepper**
½ **teaspoon seasoning salt**
1 **10¾-ounce can condensed cream of chicken soup**
2 **pie crust sticks, or other crust for two 9-inch pies**
2 **tablespoons poppy seeds**

Brown onions slightly in a skillet with shortening. Stir in ground beef and brown. Add remaining ingredients and cook until all of the liquid is gone. Let this mixture cool. Meanwhile, roll out pie crust sticks, sprinkling the poppy seeds over the dough about half-way through the rolling process in order to incorporate them into the dough. Cut 4 large or 8 smaller circles out of the dough. Spoon cooled hamburger mixture onto one side of each circle leaving a ¼-inch border of dough. Fold other end of dough over and score the edges with a fork. Bake in preheated 400-degree oven for 20 minutes or until nicely browned.

Pumpkin Bread

MAKES 2 LOAVES

Use any leftovers from this quick, sweet bread to make a pumpkin bread pudding.

3 cups sugar
4 eggs, beaten
1 16-ounce can pumpkin
1 cup vegetable oil
3½ cups all-purpose flour
2 teaspoons baking soda
1 teaspoon baking powder
2 teaspoons salt
½ teaspoon ground cloves
1 teaspoon nutmeg
1 teaspoon cinnamon
1 teaspoon allspice
⅔ cup water
½ cup chopped pecans

Preheat oven to 350 degrees. In a large bowl, combine sugar, eggs, pumpkin, and oil, mixing well. In a separate bowl, combine flour, baking soda, baking powder, salt, and spices. Gradually add dry ingredients to pumpkin mixture, alternating with water, mixing well after each addition. Add pecans. Pour into 2 greased 9x5-inch loaf pans. Bake for 1 hour or until loaf springs back when touched lightly. Do not overcook. Take out of pans and cool on a wire rack.

Sweet-Potato Muffins

MAKES 18 MUFFINS

The pecans and raisins in this recipe are optional. If you want to try something different, substitute walnuts and dried cranberries for them.

½ cup oleo
1¼ cup sugar, plus more for spinkling over the tops of the muffins
2 eggs
1¼ cup canned yams
1½ cup flour
2 teaspoons baking powder
¼ teaspoon salt
1 teaspoon cinnamon
¼ teaspoon nutmeg
1 cup milk
¼ cup chopped pecans
½ cup chopped raisins

Preheat oven to 400 degrees. Cream oleo, sugar, add eggs. Blend in yams. Sift flour, baking powder, salt, cinnamon, and nutmeg. Gradually stir the dry ingredients into the yam mixture, alternating with the milk. Do not over mix. Fold in pecans and raisins. Fill greased muffin tins two-thirds full with batter. Sprinkle tops with light coating of sugar. Bake 25 minutes, or until the muffins spring back when touched lightly.

Zucchini Bread

MAKES 2 LOAVES

The key to making this bread is removing all the moisture from the grated zucchini before combining all the ingredients.

2 cups grated zucchini
3 eggs
1 cup vegetable oil
1½ cups sugar
2 teaspoons vanilla extract
2 cups flour, sifted
2 teaspoons baking soda
¼ teaspoon baking powder
1 tablespoon ground cinnamon
1 teaspoon salt
½ teaspoon lemon zest
1 cup chopped pecans

Preheat oven to 375 degrees. Place zucchini in a colander and press down firmly on it until you have removed all the moisture; set aside. In a large bowl, beat eggs lightly. Stir in oil, sugar, zucchini, and vanilla. Sift flour, baking soda, baking powder, cinnamon, and salt into a small bowl. Stir dry ingredients into egg mixture until well blended. Stir in lemon zest and pecans. Divide batter between two well-greased 8 x 5 x 3-inch loaf pans. Bake for 1 hour or until center springs back when lightly pressed. Cool pans on a wire rack 10 minutes, then remove bread from pans and return to rack to cool completely.

Drinks

All of the beverages described in this chapter are strictly legal unless you happen to substitute a certain, uh, libation that Uncle Jack is allegedly responsible for boiling up in that shack he's got behind the creek. Even then it's only illegal if you get caught, I suppose. The most important thing about this chapter is that we will set out to prove, once and for all, that there is life after beer.

Drinks and entertaining go hand-in-hand, so a lot of the recipes included here are perfect for parties. In particular, Caesar's Punch Bowl, Moody's Holiday Punch, and Orange Party Punch are good for big groups and will do you proud. For tamer affairs, try the Shirley Temple Punch or Sherbet Punch (anyone who requires a little proof can slip it right into their own glass).

Anytime Cocktail

MAKES 10 TO 12 DRINKS

Keep this in your icebox and serve it over ice...anytime!

12 lemons
1 fifth water
1½ cups sugar
1 fifth whiskey

Juice lemons. Boil water, add sugar, and cook until dissolved. Remove from heat and add whiskey and lemon juice. Let stand until cool. Keep refrigerated.

Caesar's Punch Bowl

MAKES 40 SERVINGS

This recipe calls for "simple syrup"; if you don't have it around, don't worry—simple is the key word here. Just take an equal amount (by volume) of water and and sugar and cook it over medium heat, stirring, until the mixture just begins to boil and all the sugar crystals are dissolved. Take it off the heat, let it cool, and there you have it.

2 cups diced pineapple
½ cup simple syrup
½ cup lemon juice
½ cup orange juice
½ cup pineapple juice
1½ cups Pearl brandy (or your favorite brandy)
2 fifths light rum
block of ice
2 quarts soda water
1 pint sliced strawberries

Place pineapple, simple syrup, fruit juices, brandy and rum in a punch bowl. Add block of ice. Pour in soda water and strawberries.

Day-Before-Payday Cocktails

SERVES 8

This cocktail is shaken together with an egg white, an old bartender's trick that gives a drink a lot of body and just a bit of foamy head. Talk about a great way to stretch out that last paycheck! (Of course, all the usual warnings about eating or drinking anything with raw egg apply here...)

9 jiggers gin
3 jiggers sweet vermouth
2 jiggers grenadine
3 lemons, juiced
1 egg white

Shake all ingredients together with crushed ice.

Derby Mint Gulp

MAKES 1 DRINK

Not just for Kentucky Derby day.

34 mint leaves
1 teaspoon sugar
1 teaspoon water
shaved ice
2 jiggers bourbon

Chill a 12-ounce glass in the freezer. When glass is well chilled, combine mint leaves, sugar, and water in glass. Fill glass with finely shaved ice. Pour in one jigger of bourbon and stir hard until ice is almost melted. Fill remainder of glass with crushed ice and pour in another jigger of bourbon. Decorate with a stem of fresh mint.

Homemade Kahlúa

MAKES ABOUT A GALLON

This is also wonderful over ice cream.

1½ cups instant coffee powder
3 cups boiling water
6 cups sugar
1 vanilla bean
fifth of vodka

Dissolve coffee in boiling water; add sugar and vanilla bean. Let cool and add vodka. Pour into a gallon jug, seal, and let stand for 30 days.

Instant Spiced Tea

MAKES ABOUT HALF A GALLON

My mother always had a jar of this heavenly treat around!

1 large (21-ounce) jar (preferably Tang™)
¾ cup presweetened instant tea mix with lemon
1½ cups sugar
1½ teaspoon ground cloves
1½ teaspoon ground cinnamon

Combine all ingredients and mix well. Use 2 coffee spoons full for each cup or glass of water—hot or cold.

Milk Punch

MAKES 1 DRINK

You'll find a lot of versions of milk punch out there, but here's a simple one that does the trick.

1½ ounces bourbon or rum
1 cup milk
1 teaspoon sugar
crushed ice

Combine ingredients in a mason jar with a lid. Shake well and pour into a glass.

Moody's Holiday Punch

SERVES 12

This hot cider recipe is great at the holidays, and so simple you don't even have to strain out the cloves and cinnamon stick if you don't want to.

8 cups sweet cider
16 whole cloves
4 cinnamon sticks
1 fifth dark rum

In a large pot, heat cider, cloves, and cinnamon sticks for 10 minutes. Turn heat to low and add rum (do not boil). Serve hot in mugs.

Orange Party Punch

SERVES 20

If you want a great party punch for a wild shindig, add 1 quart light rum to this punch.

½ cup sugar
6 cups orange juice
1 cup fresh lemon juice
½ cup maraschino cherry juice
½ gallon orange sherbet
4 cups ginger ale
orange slices topped with maraschino cherries for garnish

Dissolve sugar in fruit juices by stirring and then put into the icebox to chill. Place sherbet in punch bowl and pour fruit juices and ginger ale over sherbet. Float orange slices on top of the punch and place a cherry on top of each slice.

Sherbet Punch

MAKES 1½ GALLONS

Wow!

½ gallon rainbow sherbet
1 quart pineapple juice
1 quart orange juice
1 quart lemonade
1 quart ginger ale

Mix juices and ginger ale together. Place rainbow sherbet in a punch bowl and pour liquids around it.

Shirley Temple Punch

MAKES 2½ GALLONS

Here's a great non-alchoholic punch and another reason you should never throw out that maraschino cherry juice!

3 quarts orange juice
2 cups lemonade
1 cup maraschino cherry juice
1 cups sugar
1 gallon orange sherbet
2 quarts ginger ale
orange slices for garnish

Combine orange juice, lemonade, maraschino cherry juice, and sugar; chill. Place sherbet in a punch bowl and pour juices and ginger ale over it. Garnish with orange slices.

Tennessee Coffee

MAKES 1 DRINK

The whipped cream and cherry garnish add a fancy kick to this drink, but you can leave them out, and take your Jack and coffee straighter, if that's more your style.

3 sugar cubes
1 jigger Jack Daniel's
strong black coffee
whipped cream
cherry for garnish

Drop sugar cubes into a large, warm whiskey glass. Pour Jack Daniel's over cubes, and fill ¾ full with black coffee. Top with whipped cream (do not stir) and garnish with a cherry.

Desserts

Cousin Nadine went to some fancy-pants, big-city restaurant where they served up a piece of cake that looked just like a piano. Well, fancy that. It sure sounds real pretty but who the heck would want to eat a piano? You can keep all the frills and doo-dads. There are only two things in this world that can truly be described as delicious hunks. One is Billy Ray Cyrus and the other is a piece of cake. Now that I think about it, pudding and pie run neck-'n-neck in the yummy category also.

Around here, convenience foods like Cool Whip, Jell-O, store-bought angel food cake, and even Twinkies are pretty near classic ingredients when it come to dessert making, and many of the recipes below reflect this. Others, like Apple Skillet Cake and Kentucky Bourbon Cake, are country favorites and a bit more rustic. Both styles find favor in this neck of the woods and always please friends and family.

Apple Skillet Cake

SERVES 6

Skillet cakes are very popular in these parts. Don't hesitate to substitute other fruit in season—peaches, cherries, or even canned fruits—for the apples in this recipe. Just remember to adjust the quantity of sugar if your fruit is particularly tart or sweet.

1½ cups flour
1 teaspoon baking soda
1 teaspoon salt
1 cup sugar
¾ cup salad oil
½ cup buttermilk
1 egg
2 apples, peeled, cored, and sliced
1 teaspoon vanilla extract
1 cup chopped pecans

Preheat oven to 350 degrees. Sift together flour, baking soda, salt, and sugar. Add remaining ingredients and mix well. Pour batter into lightly greased, 10-inch cast-iron skillet and bake for 40 to 50 minutes, or until the cake springs back when lightly touched in the center and just begins to pull away from the sides of the skillet. Serve warm with butter or whipped cream.

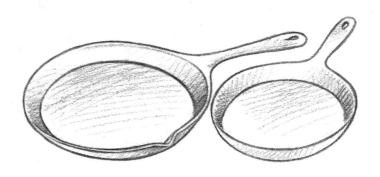

Billy's Sweet-Potato Pie

SERVES 8

The grape jelly and meringue on this pie are kind of unusual—I guess that's the way Billy likes it—but it's a pretty good recipe even if you want to omit them (if you do, just add the eggs whole to the pie filling without separating them).

1½ cups cooked sweet potatoes
½ cup milk
2 eggs, separated
1 cup plus 2 tablespoons sugar
½ teaspoon cinnamon
¼ teaspoon nutmeg
1 9-inch unbaked pie shell
grape jelly

Preheat oven to 375 degrees. Cream potatoes with milk. Beat in egg yolks and 1 cup of the sugar. Add cinnamon and nutmeg and pour into unbaked pie shell. Bake until set, about 45 to 55 minutes. Remove pie from oven and lower oven temperature to 300 degrees. Spread the top of pie with a thin layer of grape jelly. Beat egg whites and remaining 2 tablespoons of sugar in a dry, clean bowl until it holds stiff peaks. Cover pie with meringue and return pie to oven. Bake for 15 to 20 minutes, or until meringue is lightly browned.

Bessie's Fudge Squares

MAKES 12 LARGE SQUARES

These rich, unleavened brownies are lovely on their own or served with vanilla ice cream, but chocolate icing puts them over the top. Overbaking will make them dry, so watch them carefully.

1 stick (½ cup) butter
4 1-ounce squares unsweetened baking chocolate
4 eggs
2 cups sugar
1 cup cake flour
¼ teaspoon salt
2 cups chopped pecans
1 tablespoon vanilla extract

Preheat oven to 350 degrees. Melt butter with chocolate in the top of a double boiler set over simmering water; set aside. Beat eggs, add sugar and mix well. Add flour and salt and mix well. Stir in pecans and vanilla. Add chocolate mixture and mix well. Pour batter into a greased and floured 12x9x2-inch baking pan and bake for 35 minutes, or until a toothpick inserted in the center of the pan comes out almost clean (do not overbake). Invert pan onto a cooling rack; once cool, ice the brownies with with Chocolate Icing for Bessie's Fudge Squares *(recipe below)* and cut into 12 squares.

Chocolate Icing for Bessie's Fudge Squares

MAKES ENOUGH ICING FOR 12 SQUARES

1 stick (½ cup) butter
1 egg
2½ cups powdered sugar
2 1-ounce squares unsweetened baking chocolate, melted
1 teaspoon vanilla extract

Cream butter until light and fluffy; add egg and sugar and beat hard. Add melted chocolate and vanilla. Continue beating until smooth and firm enough to spread.

Bubble Ring

SERVES 8

These will make your house smell heavenly. Cut this recipe in half if you only own one Bundt pan.

2 sticks (1 cup) oleo
½ cup brown sugar
pecans (chopped or whole, and as many as you like)
1 package (24) frozen hot rolls
1 cup granulated sugar
1 tablespoon cinnamon

Have 2 Bundt pans ready. Melt one stick of the oleo and the brown sugar in a small pan set over medium heat. Stir in the pecans and divide the mixture between the two Bundt pans, spreading it evenly over the bottoms. In a small skillet, melt the remaining stick of oleo. In a bowl mix together granulated sugar and cinnamon. Roll frozen rolls in oleo, then in cinnamon sugar. Put rolls standing on end into Bundt pan and let them sit out on your kitchen counter overnight. Next morning, bake the rolls in a preheated 350-degree oven for 30 minutes. Let cool before turning out of pan

Chocolate Twinkie Pie

SERVES 6

I make this for the kids when they bring home their report cards. You have to reward the hard work, and they love it!

12 Twinkies®, each cut into 4 pieces horizontally
3 eggs, separated
1 6-ounce package semisweet chocolate chips, melted
½ cup sugar
1 teaspoon vanilla extract
1 cup chopped pecans
2 cups Cool Whip® or sweetened whipped cream

Line a baking dish with half of the Twinkies. Beat egg yolks and add to melted chocolate. Combine egg whites with sugar and vanilla and whip until they hold stiff peaks. Gently fold egg whites into chocolate mixture and pour half over Twinkies. Sprinkle top with half of the chopped pecans. Make another layer of Twinkies, chocolate, and pecans. Top with Cool Whip. Cover and refrigerate overnight.

Coconut Ice Cream Balls

SERVES 6

This is one of my favorites!

2 pints vanilla ice cream
2 to 3 cups shredded coconut

Using an ice cream scoop, make balls out of the ice cream and place on a cookie sheet covered with coconut. Roll balls in coconut until they are covered and return them quickly to the freezer until ready to serve. Place one or two balls in a bowl and splash with Homemade Kahlúa (*see page 106*) over the top.

Cornflake Ring with Ice Cream Balls

SERVES 12

This one is great when the whole family comes over and it is beautiful!

1½ cups brown sugar
2 tablespoons light Karo® corn syrup
½ cup milk
½ stick (¼ cup) butter or oleo
2 cups cornflakes
vanilla ice cream

In a small, heavy saucepan, mix brown sugar, corn syrup, milk, and butter. Cook over medium heat until a soft ball forms when you spoon a bit of the hot mixture into cold water. Place cornflakes in a large mixing bowl and pour the hot syrup over and mix lightly. Pack cornflakes gently into a greased ring mold. Let cool on the counter for a while and then cover with wax paper until ready to serve.

When ready to serve, turn cornflake ring onto a large platter. Place balls of vanilla ice cream all around and in the center of the ring. For a little something extra, pour on some chocolate sauce!

Fruit and Jell-O Mold

SERVES 8

You don't have to think of this as just a dessert. A lot of folks make this mold and serve it at the holidays in place of cranberry relish.

3 cups raw cranberries
3 large seedless oranges, unpeeled
1 cup sugar
2 3-ounce packages lemon Jell-O®
2 cups boiling water
2 cups ice water

Grind cranberries and unpeeled oranges coarsely in a meat grinder. Add sugar and set aside. Dissolve Jell-O in boiling water and stir in ice water. Pour Jell-O into a ring mold sprayed with Pam and set in the icebox. Check the Jell-O after 1 hour; if the mixture has started to thicken, gently stir in the ground fruit. Return the Jell-O to the icebox and chill until set, about 5 hours or overnight. Unmold on a platter covered with lettuce leaves and serve with mayonnaise.

Helen's Coconut Cake

SERVES 8 TO 10

Rich and fabulous!

1 box white cake mix, prepared and baked according to package directions
1 8¾-ounce can sweetened coconut milk
1 14-oz can sweetened and condensed Eagle® Brand milk
Cool Whip®
1 7-ounce package coconut, frozen

Mix and bake your favorite white cake mix according to directions on box. Leave the cake in the pan, and while it is still hot use the handle of a wooden spoon to poke lots of holes over the top of the cake. Pour coconut milk and then condensed milk, over cake. Let sit until cool. When cool, cover with Cool Whip® and sprinkle frozen coconut over the top.

Hershey Bar Cake

SERVES 10 TO 12

This recipe calls for Hershey bars, but you can substitute about 12 ounces of any sweetened chocolate if you like.

2 sticks (1 cup) oleo
2 cups sugar
4 eggs
2 teaspoons vanilla extract
pinch of salt
8 small (1.5-ounce) Hershey® chocolate bars, melted
2½ cups sifted flour
1 cup buttermilk
Pinch of baking soda
1 cup chopped pecans
Powdered sugar for garnish

Preheat oven to 300 degrees. Cream oleo and sugar. Add eggs one at a time, beating well after each addition. Add vanilla, salt, melted Hershey bars, flour, buttermilk mixed with baking soda, and pecans and mix until combined. Pour batter into a greased Bundt pan and bake for 1 hour and 40 minutes, or until cake just begins to pull away from the sides of the pan. Cool upside-down on a rack until cake is free from pan. Remove cooled cake from pan and sift powdered sugar over the top.

In-the-Pink Marshmallow Puddin'

SERVES 16

This unusual "puddin" is sandwiched between the layers of an angel food cake. If you don't want to buy the one they sell at your grocery store you can make your own from scratch—but honey, why bother?

2 10-ounce bags marshmallows
2 10-ounce bottles maraschino cherries
2 cups pecan pieces
1 cup bourbon
1 pint whipping cream
1 angel food cake

With kitchen scissors, cut marshmallows into bite-size pieces. Drain cherries (but save that juice!) and chop them coarsely, reserving a few cherries for decoration. Combine marshmallows, chopped cherries, and pecans in a large bowl. Pour cherry juice and bourbon over mixture. Cover and let stand overnight in the icebox, stirring several times. When ready to serve, whip cream until it forms soft peaks and fold half of it into the pudding mixture. Cut angel food cake into two layers and spread pudding mixture in between the layers. Ice cake with additional whipped cream and decorate with cherries.

Kentucky Bourbon Cake

SERVES 20

Store these cakes in a cool, dry place (Granny kept hers in the linen closet) and they will keep almost indefinitely.

¾ pound (3 sticks) butter
2 cups sugar
6 eggs
½ cup molasses

4 cups flour
1 heaping teaspoon baking powder
2 teaspoons ground nutmeg
1 pound raisins
1 cup chopped candied pineapple
1 cup chopped candied cherries
1 cup orange marmalade
2 pounds chopped pecans
1 cup bourbon, plus more for soaking cakes in
2 apples, cut into ½-inch slices

Preheat oven to 250 degrees. Cream butter and sugar and add eggs, one at a time, beating well after each addition. Add molasses and mix well. In another bowl, sift together flour, baking powder, and nutmeg. Put raisins, pineapple, cherries, marmalade, and pecans in large bowl. Stir 1 cup of flour mixture into the fruit. Gradually add remainder of flour to egg mixture, alternating with bourbon. Stir in the fruit and nut mixture. Grease 2 large loaf pans and line them with greased brown paper (you can cut up grocery bags). Pour batter into pans and cover with the end of brown paper. Bake for 2½ to 3 hours, until a toothpick inserted in the center of the cakes comes out clean. Let cakes cool 10 minutes before removing them from the pans, then cool completely on a wire rack.

When cooled, wrap each cake in a cloth napkin which has been dampened with bourbon. Place wrapped cakes in a tin container, spread apple slices over them, cover, and allow to sit 3 to 4 weeks before eating. If you want to go all out, open tin once a week and dampen napkins with more bourbon.

Lemon Angel Food Cake

SERVES 8

This molded gelatin dessert has a lot of peoples' favorites in it—lemons, angel food cake, and Cool Whip—so maybe that accounts for its popularity. It's a crowd pleaser, so don't be put off by having to cook over a double boiler for a few minutes.

juice of 6 lemons
1 tablespoon gelatin
peel from 3 lemons, grated
6 eggs, separated
1½ cups sugar
1 angel food cake
Cool Whip® or whipped cream for garnish

Heat lemon juice until hot, but don't let it boil. Dissolve gelatin in the hot lemon juice and let cool. Beat together lemon juice, grated peel, egg yolks, and ¾ cup of the sugar. Pour mixture into the top of a double boiler set over simmering water and cook until mixture starts to thicken and the sugar is melted. Allow to cool. In a another bowl, beat the egg whites and remaining ¾ cup sugar until it holds stiff peaks. Fold egg whites into the lemon mixture. Break angel food cake into bite-size pieces and gently fold it into the lemon mixture. Pour into a 3-quart casserole that has been lightly sprayed with Pam and refrigerate until set, 6 to 8 hours or overnight. Unmold and garnish with Cool Whip.

Mississippi Mud Cake

SERVES 6 TO 8

The secret to keeping this very dense cake moist is not to overbake it. Watch it carefully, and err on the side of underbaking if you must. For a thicker cake, bake this recipe in a 9-inch round cake pan; you can line the pan with strips of wax paper to make it easier to unmold.

FOR THE CAKE

1¾ cups sugar
1¾ cups self-rising flour
⅓ cup unsweetened cocoa powder
⅓ cup vegetable oil
4 eggs, beaten
3 teaspoons vanilla extract
2 cups nuts
1 7½-ounce jar marshmallow cream

FOR THE ICING

1 cup granulated sugar
¼ cup cocoa
½ cup milk
1 stick (½ cup) butter or oleo
powdered sugar

To make the cake, preheat oven to 350 degrees. Mix all ingredients together and bake in 13x9-inch greased and floured pan for 35 to 40 minutes, or until the cake just starts to pull away from the sides of the pan and a toothpick inserted into the center of the cake comes out almost clean. Invert the cake onto a cooling rack and spread marshmallow cream over the top while it's still warm.

To make the icing, place all ingredients except the powdered sugar in a saucepan and bring them to a boil over medium-high heat, stirring often. Boil for 3 minutes, remove pan from heat, and allow icing to cool slightly. Beat in powdered sugar until the icing is as thick as you like it. Spread over top of cooled cake.

Peppermint Chiffon Pie

SERVES 8

This is a very pretty and fluffy dessert. You can make this during the holidays if you got a bunch of those candy canes lying around. Actually, you can always use those white-and-red striped mints they give out at the diner for the peppermint flavor.

½ cup crushed peppermint sticks
½ cup sugar
1 envelope gelatin
1¼ cups milk
3 eggs, separated
¼ teaspoon salt
1 or 2 drops red food coloring
3 egg whites
1 graham cracker crust
½ cup canned whipped cream (like Reddi Wip®),
plus more for garnish

Mix candy, ¼ cup of the sugar, gelatin, milk, egg yolks, and salt until well combined. Cook in the top of a double boiler set over simmering water until gelatin dissolves and candy melts. Remove from the heat, tint with a drop or two of food coloring, and chill the mixture until partially set.

Beat egg whites until stiff. Gradually add ¼ cup sugar. Fold egg whites into the cooled gelatin mixture. Fold in the ½ cup whipped cream and pile the mixture into the graham cracker crust. Chill. When ready to serve top with more whipped cream.

Toffee Ice Cream Pie

SERVES 8

Hot chocolate sauce puts this dessert over the top. But if you're not up for the extra cooking (and we all understand that), just serve the pie on its own.

FOR THE PIE

1¼ cups chocolate wafer crumbs
½ stick (¼ cup) butter, melted
12 small Heath® bars
½ gallon vanilla ice cream

FOR THE CHOCOLATE SAUCE

1 stick (½ cup) butter
1 12-ounce package semisweet chocolate chips
2 cups powdered sugar
1 12-ounce can evaporated milk
2 teaspoons vanilla extract

To make the pie, mix chocolate wafer crumbs and melted butter and transfer to a 13x8-inch pan. Pat crust down evenly over bottom of pan and put it in the refrigerator to harden. Refrigerate Heath bars to harden them and then crush them. Soften ice cream and mix with Heath bars. Spoon ice cream mixture into crust and let stand in the freezer overnight.

To make the chocolate sauce, melt butter and chocolate chips in the top of a double boiler set over simmering water. Transfer chocolate mixture to a saucepan and stir in powdered sugar and evaporated milk. Cook over medium heat, stirring, for about 8 minutes or until thickened. Remove from heat, stir in vanilla, and serve warm over pie.

Index